Prairie Harbour

Also by Garry Thomas Morse

POETRY
   After Jack*
   Discovery Passages*
   Streams
   Transversals for Orpheus

FICTION
   Death in Vancouver*
   Minor Episodes / Major Ruckus*
   Minor Expectations*
   Rogue Cells / Carbon Harbour*

*Available from Talonbooks

PRAIRIE HARBOUR

GARRY
THOMAS
MORSE

TALONBOOKS

Talonbooks
278 East First Avenue, Vancouver, British Columbia, Canada v5T 1A6
www.talonbooks.com

First printing: 2015

Printed and bound in Canada on 100% post-consumer recycled paper
Interior and cover design by Typesmith
On the cover: Agnes Martin, *Wheat* (1957), oil on canvas
© Estate of Agnes Martin / SODRAC (2015); courtesy the Doris and Donald
Fisher Collection at the San Francisco Museum of Modern Art
Photograph reproduced courtesy Pace Gallery, New York

Talonbooks acknowledges the financial support of the Canada Council for
the Arts, the Government of Canada through the Canada Book Fund, and the
Province of British Columbia through the British Columbia Arts Council and
the Book Publishing Tax Credit.

LIBRARY AND ARCHIVES CANADA CATALOGUING IN PUBLICATION

Morse, Garry Thomas, author
        Prairie harbour / Garry Thomas Morse.

Poems.
ISBN 978-0-88922-940-2 (PAPERBACK)
        I. Title.

PS8626.O774P73 2015   C811'.6   C2015-904157-0

Though they are blazoned in the poet's song
As all the comforts which our lives contain
I read and sought such joys my whole life long
And found the best of poets sung in vain
But still I read and sighed and sued again

— JOHN CLARE

agile
Allard's
Arizona
black-legged
black-sided
Bradley's
Brownsville
Caribbean
carinate
common
delicate
dusky-faced
Eurasian
gladiator
graceful
Gulf
handsome
lesser pine
long-spurred
long-tailed
military
nimble
Pacific
prairie
red-headed
saltmarsh
San Diego
seashore
seaside
short-winged
slender
spotted-legged
straight-lanced
stripe-faced
superb
Texas
tidewater
wingless
woodland

*Meadow katydids north of Mexico

PRAIRIE
HARBOUR
1–12

It is not place alone that matters but a direction, an attraction —
something like the movement of a compass needle; not where it is, but where
it points matters. My image for the prairie writer then ... is not necessarily
the one who is in the west, or who stays here, but the one who
returns, who moves, who points in this direction.

— ELI MANDEL

Native of this have-
not province, old flame
speak through the flame
as you may much later

whether Anglo-
Saxon or Late Renaissance depiction, with the Angel
helping or helping too much (no scribe
left behind) what I prefer is Simone
Martini's *Annunciation* in gold
leaf
& that peevish look of please
take it away, that undercooked supper
or glint
of eroticism through crassness
we find in Klimt
that wardrobe
malfunction of Judith or swollen
head
of Holofernes a home
of mud
(& wattles pending ...)
in this sod-
turning work
does not make
one-eighth of eightplex
said to be
on the mayor's land
& made up first
said to sink
into foundation
before we are
devoured by
voles
(or vowels?)
drowning, not waving, sorrows in this dry flat land, wringing out
remnants of what will no longer cohere

here,   waiting
for you like Saskatchewan, for the "boom"
to blast
me out into cadmium
bloom

that is hardly fair when this is a relatively

clean slate with only letters
& disparate histories
     snowblanded out
eyes in downtown
  library self-
   censoring
     swollen tit
     (& head)

     but December is the darkest month
     but February is the present moon
     three-quarters
       full
when the rabbits are white-
    tailed hares
    rolled into
     near-invisible
  balls
storing solar gifts
for sake of imminent
madness
   (this would get a prestigious
  nod
   if only the Inuit hunter
       would shatter
that hunk of
   labradorite
    & let out the aching
       aurora borealis
with all its green
   monoculture
     tourists in the tundra
     make love to
       presumably with an
       inukshuk stopwatch)

  but if labradorite
  were breathed softly
  onto condo wall
  in vermilion
  it might get real

                              shape-
                              shifting quick
                              as jackrabbits
jumping
              out of
                          forms
to forage
              & ruminate forbs
                                    while that raven (stereo-
                                          typical Creator figure)
                          becomes curmudgeonly
                                          at noon
                    trying to eat his tiny
                    sandwich in peace
                    along Gordon Road
                                          where our goofs
                                                & mispronunciations
                    proudly flap in wind
                    chill, soon become
                                    gospel
notwithstanding
I have been rather pig-
headed & staticky as
old old-school hieratics

              speak to me then

                          of trees on your farm
                          of succulent saskatoons
                          of visions in perfect colour
                          of music in crystalline
                                          reflections

              speak through the flame

                                          & I will forgo
                    spectres
                          plaguing Europe
                                    & shadows cast
                                          across "primitive" minds
& concerti in the kaffeeklatsch
where even a secular musical
orgasm could not secure
a spot
              wiping tables

                    or a decent gig
          in the Fatherland
                                        those two women, bare
                                        armed in black dresses
                                        handle
                                                  hanks of horse-
                                        hair, stroke
                                                       interstellar
                                        violas
          these Zukofskyisms
          have no bearing on
          our oral tradition
          our conquest by
                    "sensuous genius"
          after glaciation
                    when fish were fish
          the guts that
          were ripped out
                    in the time of shamans
          the birth of a
                    dust bowl
          the promises
                    like all pamphleture
          between teeth

                                        speak to me at long last

                                        speak through flame

here I rove
          butteless in the cold
                              covering
                                        provincial wiseacres
then back to
          prairie "harbour"

                    still waiting
                    for that
                    blasted
                    stone
                    to
                              cleave

More reverb:
movement from Mass.
to La Nouvelle-Écosse
Edison
& Bell
(pick up
pick up
hence our retreat
into primal
telegraphy
(charged per minute by Tesla?)
but what
about these terrestrial
emanations

not spirits, per
se   but echoes
of doings
ridged
impressions
across land-
scape
bones
buried
deep in the flat-
earth society

speak
when all your talk
of treaties
& conquest
has taken
the floor
from under
speak
when you
have taken
apart the intricate
mechanics of
affect
or for that matter
molecular advances
in raw emoting

                speak
                        then set those words
                                down   (words a Mohawk
                                                elder in a book
                                                thought more
                                                        dry *excrement*)

        speak when the Large
        Hadron Collider
        finally appropriates
        our space with a tiny
        black hole from the
        fifth or eleventh
        dimension

                                then get the *Leader-*
                                Post on the horn
                                & tell 'em
                                suo motu
                                cognizance
                                        the
                                poet is making
                                the land grab
                                for once

        meanwhile back
        in Morse Cemetery
        that plaque makes
        'em the parents
        of Nova Scotia

                        planters who
                        came from
                        Boston in the
                        Charming Molly
                        in 1760

                                [quite a *Heritage*
                                        Minute, hey]

                but the briny
                ocean tossed
                is not here
                neither heave
                nor sigh of it

        rather the body imbued with strange
        energy at the hour of holding vigil
        knows more than I do, much as
        hidden hares know more than I do

Flakes,   motes
   slough   of skin
history,   memory
   please   only
                  speak
                     when the present
                                    moment
      strikes you as
                  finitely
                     appealing
unless epidemic
lack of learning means
the inability to modify
beef
      & prolong
            milk
                        then puzzle   then puzzle
                        over every   over every
                        apparatus   promise of
                        that alters   knowledge
                        ALL   & even
                                                     love
                  passed over like trembling Tettigoniidae

                  while rabbits
                  throw off
                  unsociability
                              & eye one
                                    another
                  over herbivore
                  voracity
                              that sunlit eye
                              portentous of
                              the next moon

on the land reserve that leads to the #1
                                    & then nothing
but last night
                        a face
            through gate
                        peering,   listening
            then slipping
                              through
                                    & then nothing

sailing over
                on the *Charming Molly*
to Annapolis County
with two oxen, two
cows, and one horse
                        not quite
                        getting Anna
                            or Abner
                                        dashing, maybe a bit
                                        dotty, of the G_d-
                                        mad Morses from Mass.
                                        wondering
                        in horse
                                    what
                        hath Morse
                                    wrought

        Annapolis is this

but it would befit one of their heirs
apparent to treat this humid plain
like exilic hermitage
                        out of Black Sea
when there is only shallow slough
packed with epistles
                        begging pardons
                        in a hundred
                        or so poems
                        in hundreds
                            & hundreds
                                of poems
even old
        flame(s)
                    picking us up
                                    along Island Highway
    where ancestral
seat
        quietly sinks
            into shadow
                            (it was never
                            ours to begin
                            with, nothing
                            was, matters)
chastened over rod
caught in planks

where that giant
stone
    eXplODeD
          over ebb
      tide
              love-
           making
              for passing
                cruise liners

        stars
     rippling
         in the
           Nimpkish

that is not spirits
but doings in
the balloon animal
shape of longings

burst
    into being
        & have I not stolen away
        until a time of reckoning
        with these fetching things

        under my arm

         in this ornate
         box of light

3

Or flames,
oriflammes on days
the sky shows
no clemency
stories about
folks crying
in the
downtown
library
in no
connection
with the RSO
demonstration
losing someone
to hand strain
poems about
perishing
instead of
publishing
in cold
grey
square

taken away by clusters
of tempo   contrasts
of forte   pianissimo

rests   between   phrases

having occasion to gloss my own dying tongue
whenever the mood strikes me
yet that restless wanderlust
is a told tale
& sags
about the eyes
& lingers
like a foot on the sostenuto
pedal
riding away with flowery skirt in bloom

what sticks out in this issue is verse
from at least four other editors
of literary magazines

reading in the paper just the other day
you need to stop & I need to stop
or at least to slow down & stop
thinking we're so ha-ha funny
with all these words in books
that sell paper but not papers
all these communal musings
that somehow lack Toronto

do you think such scratch-me-back
gets by our eyes, the few of us there are
who read?

writer, what to write
maybe quaint mornings
when a pristine blanket of
ice crystals
            encourages the eye

        or evidence of
        dirty-faced hares
        soiling them-
                    selves
                silly
                    so why did you come here
then a grin
            at sometimes grim
        faces
            surprised by someone
                            on foot
        or surprised to be
                    caught inside
                            that swerving
                                groaning
                                fuming
                                    thing
                    ah, *sustain*
each of these "strains" lacking class
of mutually consensual commerce
when running in sudden bursts
through snowdrifts –
                    the necessary
fright of our lives
                    for a second
            rousing

rabbits
            & myself
                    out of the kind
                    of complacency
                    Catullus warns
                    us against
                              still lacking
                              "agribition" to
                              pen erotic
                              potboiler
                              about
                                      seed
                                    banks

that involves passing through Morse,   SK
on the way to Forget, as Kiyooka might
call to mind
                  along with his greens
                  in MacKenzie gallery

Mere hours or eons
later, do you stomach
these oriflammes past
their shelf life,   these
dusty old sweets
                in gut

                            best to press
                                      down
                          on the pedal
                                          pocket them
                              for later

4

Or
                non-
            flames
        a
    retraction
                for aforementioned
                vivaciousness
                        is pending ...
however, the
voice that once
reached each corner
of that lonely square
will with difficulty
surrender, nay
suppress that
            URGENCY
                    that since the 1930s
                    all members of the
                    Regina Symphony
                    Women's Association
                    have felt it
                        obbligato
        for a bit of a "birdseye"
        to hear the Concerto in B
        Minor for Four Violins &
        Cello from
                L'Estro Armonico

only then within the confines of this perimeter
    / sunlight shining through trees /
could an orderly chase be said to begin
                    why
        only yesterday
                there were two
        hummingbirds
                sucking the honey
                        of music vows

            [unless that is honeysuckle
                        on a thank-
                    you card from
                    Montreal]
                        unless we think our-

selves hero to grapple
with the Aeolic
                              (or more
like funnily made
gyro
              in clever stomach):

          ] dear undark [   ] with some luck
               hold [the harbour]   pitch [soil]
          seafarers [unsure]   magnificent gusts
             on dry land   sail   burdensome
          since   [in flux]   many [shipments]
               [deeds]   dry land [

                              wait, are those plovers
                              or sanderlings or what
                              through snow-
                                             fall
                         moving as
                                   one

no
          this picnic table's from Staples
from a previous poem
                              & yes
          my light is on
                         but that won't
          deter mature
                         rabbits
from rending
                         that twiggy
                         stuff right
                         outside
                              before spring
                                        maybe
                                        if in the uniform
                                   flow of traffic downtown
                                        then elsewhere
                                             again
                                                  a breath(ing)

μεγάλαις ἀήται[ς
                         could be carefully held for
                         underpinnings of that
                         continuo
                                   that blink

of brief
intimacy
dropped
like so much ash
outside that survivor
of celebrity "cyclone"

while two ravens
<say Huginn & Muninn>
call out
overhead
each to each
commentary
on the relevance
of such
brio
in modern
times, in
perpetual
emptiness
in front of
memorial, save
for the guy with
some kind of First
Nations-specific
Tourette's
& his
kneejerk
slur
is the first
recognition
in a long time
whispering with whistle-
blower about the proud
initiative to reduce
the number of
chairs in the
library
beating lusty
retreat
back to
flat Martello tower
of the flawed
mind (whose mind?)

                    instilling insistent pulsating light
on a nearby
             crane
             with
             spare
                        thoughts
             for this, my
             own February
             personage
when in the
             concerto
in that infamous D minor (always
                            significant)
          for two violins
                    & cello
                              out of nowhere
                         that mood-
                              altering
                                    fugue
builds
          that was not the nightingales or
          shades of Callimachus, those inky
          birds, but all the same, they were
          sent out
               with the solemn hope
                                    they would
                         one day
                                    return

Flame,
    forgot again, past barking dogs on Robinson
then up to 13th Avenue
  to get the labradorite
      flat   palm
      under
then
  breathings
    that evoke the place
    of so many sighs

  reminder of reeds
  & whistles that
  announce spirits
  in the tradition
      the woman asks
      if I might want
      the little white
      prescription:
mystical & protective stone
clears & protects the aura
  the intuition
helps one access the   omitted is apotropaic
unconscious mind   totem against detractors
banishes fears & gives   rival healers, fr-
strength   enemies, guts
aids in clear thinking   ripped out at worst
helps through times of change times of
relieves stress   *affect*
good for the metabolism
lowers blood
pressure

     speaking metrically
     there is no moon
     this morning only
     flecks glints in
         stone
     beside lamp
  along with the migratory
  horses of Pech (from *puèg* lenga
  Merle   d'òc for "hill")
    their staccato

over-
lap
of controversial
dots
DNA
EVIDENCE
ABSOPROVES OUR
LACK OF
IMAGINATION
& the *New*
York Times
concurs

glissando ...   if you do not hear
slipping inside   that persistent non-
that rusted   sound right before
door   dawn

this is where
fantasie stroked
itself to life   a
hand clasp in
closed dive   a
family of fiddlers
blazing with
synesthesia
& magnificent   then a fellow pointed
gusts   out that lyric
of the small   memory is something
dark one   else

signs of varie-
gated stones
stirring in
palms, words
lolling about
cracked lips

only there is no
where to meet
& not without serious
circumspection or
delimiters
{ interruptions }

after jury duty,   a Regina
man more than intimating his
intimacy with jail-
bait

while abrupt
violin
progression
is smooth as Glass
pinching five seconds
of Verdi
evaporating
whorls
where ownership
was
eager
to unfold   to pry
that embryonic   stone
from moist
palm   to free
glints of
green

        Conjure forth
whatever
      Bachelard is on about ...
                   reverie ... hmm ...
only it is sheer
hypothesis her fingers
have moved forward
       to the fourth
movement of the fourth
suite for cello
    (Casals)
       finding forgiveness
      in that soulful
          sarabande
    (unaccompanied)
                 the jaunty
              gigue
                   never
              quite
                 reached
  also receding,   the
  shamanic motif   the
  stately lather of another
    conference on our national
              shpilkes
           under threat
or if you play it backwards, the
              prairie long poem
is totes toes up
      no art lawful
      as repeating
      oneself
        casting long shadow
    past February
          to spend
             ~~years~~ decades
          obsessed
             with something
      that may be
    a picture or
    graph of a mind
       moving

rising after
nap licking
lips to re-
read your ~~dear~~
dead letter
            (unkissed!)
yet
  the splatter
        -ed   water-
              melon
or shatter
            -ed
                  bottle   { subject
from childhood   formation }
                  would not form a
                        single
                              fugal
                                    subject
                              (for years i lived in amity horror
                                    near Main,   waiting
                              for that melon to return from lane
                                    a negative vector in physics diagram
                              when all this time you were talking
                                    about "real"
                                                lemons –
                        it's like that look on
                        Brahms's face
                                    often)
then
again
rather
long
ears
rise
            racing across little bridge
                                                chasing one of the white-
                                          tailed hares
                                                      to keep him/her
                                          & my people
                                                      spry with night
                                          terrors
      the veritable loon of "prairie harbour," taking
      neighbourhood with me in mystical hours
      but at least

the little bridge
                              between us
      is not yet part of operatic
                              immolation scene

      no, there is always room
      on this figment of a porch
      in minus
      thirty
            with wind chill
                        emoji

the running gag that once off
what an estimable colleague
calls "the hamster
            wheel"
                              retirement has
                              never been so
                              effing busy
      shhh ... observing that
                        a
                  hare
                        stopped in the
                  clover & quaking flower-
                  bells & said its prayer through
                              the rainbow
                                    across the spider's
                                    web

      that habitual steak
      sandwich kept in foil
      or balmy archive
                  the professor
      & i are going
                  to shred
            the way
                  companies
                        shred their
                        hi-
                  stories
                        (the way Brahms burned
                        all his false starts
                        & the three Schumann
                        diaries
                              if only he could!)

or in drear confession
(not that kind)
                    i don't know
                    Hegel from the bagel
                              & babka
          in my old haunt
                         (the honour my poems
                         can be used as pickup
                         lines by others
                         is yours?)
          graphing the discreet
                         mathematics of
                         horndogging

while here
          the grid
has not quite caught up
with us
          & cabbies
                    metered to the
                                   four winds
               hunt for their
                         fares
                              (a Native sage would say
                              that four is the
                              number of
                              "completeness"
                         brutally
                         unlucky
                              for others)
running, rushing, as if to find
you past
               that team
                    of hulking
     Ticats,   flirts
                    deflated
          by clueless
            landing
                    annonce
                         cet équipe
                                        on the other side of
                    that airport
                    that confused
                         scrum

or re-enact a scene
from a film
someone not bad
looking
losing at squash
unless by now the mythology
is tough as knotted sheets
no one sleeps tonight
while talk of
it recoils off
greige walls
even to admit it never
stopped ... bah ... this
übermenschy
kitschy echo of such deeply
encoded
morselogos
cannot implicate
any literal notion
of a self
[even picking up junk
calls from Scotiabank
during frozen dinner*]
positively slathered
in *Dasein*
through salad
days sneezeguard
no, in this
reverie
let us simply agree
Goethe
& Ludwig Van
walked around
"nobles"
differently
(yet Reverdy in someone's
pocket is a fabrication)

unless that *reverie*
was once bittersweet
refrain
unless by now the mythology
is that one morning

* "frozen dinner" is solely rhetorical flourish or very sad hyperbole

                    i sat down
                              to banquet table
      & wrote it all off

                                   & then

                                   never

                                   anything

7

Grouse
     or prairie
  chickens
     on this quiet jetty   the odd jet
     like a
     still from
     La Jetée

why this image persists
why this tidy
     hole in a public wall
tantalizes
     with polite introductory

    →

     where ideality
     is unexpected, more soft
     treatment
     more hands-on
     management
nothing too
sinister in
this trust-
     fall

moving from one phenomenological glom
  to another   Giacometti's grey people in
  Rothko's *Underground Fantasy*   the lady checking out
     the paper reader
     for life

yes, on second thought
this is what we slaver
     over
this attractive distance
this remote touching
     over
time, needless of much
else
     only conviction it can
     & does subsist
     meanwhile ...
(a log truck poops by
     the size of our laughter)
     yesterday

standing out of the
            fumes
                    crying   I
                                DON'T
                        KNOW
to the underdressed lady
                    in thin gloves
& sneakers
            about the North Express
                            & she smiles
                                because it is so cold
                                        & I am a
                            strange man
        (unbeknownst to her binding my own
        golden bough to a bag of nutrients

        & debating with it every day, begging
        it to fully live out its lovely damn life)
                                    & off she goes
                                    till we resume this one-
                                    act comedy in our
                                    repertoire another
                                                    time
                    the lady from the nightly
        news is about the same,   hurrying away
                                with her goodies
                    through cheaply rank   per-
                                            fumes
                    found in every Company store
                    from sea to shining sea

then to the left,   a
glint of my sudden end   (ek-
        phrastic of course)
                making the third story at six
o'clock, the community clustering
                                round
frozen
        fists clutching scribbly papers
                            (these poems!)
with a couple
        dozen
    jackrabbits

bearing the bier

        then to the right,   a
guy in the mall saying to his girl
he wants to remove a soup
can from charitable
            display
      & see the
  whole
     thing
come
    tumbling
       down

no music
no transport

mumble through this jumble
of the explicitly unwanted
                                        a
mere pang, deepening
into pain
                                exposed like so
when these empty
envelopes bring
                        mild solace,   a
thing akin to
                        friendship

softening Kaddish or
kvetch for lost years –
                        umbilical
                                ripped out
if not leech
mouths of
                        segmented
                        sleep
then humbled by what
                is shelved
                                a small
                        depression
in half-
actualized self
this not
knowing
enough to burrow
into troglodytic
                                inklings
                more distant
visions of flatlands
                                & March hares
then humbled by what
                is oppositional
                        magic

                  fingers
                        unclench,   open
                              show what looks like
                                    nothing to the naked eye
while Rilke stares right through me
guessing we are both
                  off the hook
            save for the
                  Fluß-
                        Gott
                              des Bluts
            constantly
                        churning, then blown
                                    alive upon cave
                                                wall
            like we need this reminder
            even *the eye that sticks with rime*
            cannot quite close to the fact
            we live in this world where
            Seneca will always open
                              his veins
            while hemlock is always
            exploring your options
            in one form
                        or another
            in one land
                        or another

or other elucidations in "A":

            It wouldn't do at any time
            For some Northwest Coast Indian
            To re-collect *Be* as an archetype of bees
            And neglect his *to not-be* –
            A verb which he has –

                              okay, the angsty last
            movement
                  of the Second Partita
                              for Solo Violin may be about
            something more than the loss
            or mismanagement (lest mis-
                        appropriation come into it)
            of some words
            always questionable

from the get-

go

this was a mechanical

beast

heaving, shuddering

under the brunt

of its own

comely stuffing

when a book arrived from McNally
about a girl with a birthmark in the
shape of a hare & such

accidentals

appear to be

multiplying

ah! to suck irksome thorn out
& relapse into Regina

blowing dust
from heaps
of books
that
collect
themselves

or classic

image

dropping

manuscript

onto trash

fire

like the frozen poet in

La Bohème

(ultimately the stuffed

shirt in

La Rondine)

shivering,   breathing

in

particulate

Dear begloved,
　　　　　　　　　working in humble garden
plucking out weeds
　　with know-how under busybody glares
　　　　　　　　　　　　　　　there
　　　　　　　　that weird theremin
　　　　effect in the Larghetto
riffing
　　　on formerly oboe d'amore –
　　　　　　　　　　　it might have been sweet
to enjoy those five
　　　　& some minutes together, just you, me
　　　　　　　& Trevor Pinnock's digits
　　　　　　　　　　　　　　　no, the fence
lacks integrity
　　　　　　or was it something portentous
about hair
curled about
nape
　　　　　the rest
of one's life
springing
　　　there
　　　　　　mumbling, murmuring
　　　　　　　　　　　　it might have been
　　　　　　　　　　　　　　　　　anyone
reminds me of a gate
　　　　　　　　to keep out
　　　　　　island deer
　　at
　　　the
　　　　foot
of winding stairs
a few Bringhurst
books about what
the academy calls
dead white shizzle

　　　　　　　I sit here now at my sumptuous banquet
　　　　　　　table like Qùadra, pressed to sign away
　　　　　　　my conquest with customary flourish~
　　　　　　　more like promissory note to no longer
　　　　　　　haunt about thy doors or highway

look, my books
are becoming
too blooming
Germanic, just
lie back &
think of
          ink
              land

                    while we sit alone with our troubles
                    like kewpie kids or doll-
                    like Natives in Group of Seven
                    pictures, listening to parents
                    fighting
                              in another room
                    about what is best
                    for us
                              what I wonder – was it the
or is it my family   rhetors
     o   or spinners of *politike*
     t   who first figured out how to
     e   pour
     m   the tar
         still   that would occupy
              drowsing   us all
                    next to Edward
     Curtis film taken
     for documentary
                    by most tourists
                              [that Sophoclean
                                note on white-
                                board about "Dover
                                Beach" is affecting
                                even all this *affect*]
that place too lush
          & lugubrious
                    for us
to make it
          any longer
                    already hawked
                              in spirit
                                   to hard-working sea-
                                             cucumber
                                        farmers
          swapping 'em
                    with China

                                          for LARGER
                                                    longer-lasting
                                              inukshuks

        then with briefcase
        like Robbe-Grillet's
        sad watch salesman
        or Browning's Caliban
        catch the next ferry
                        (with even Charon
                              none the wiser)
                                          Shell
                                              with the S
                                          burned out,   that place
                                        a remittance man's
                                                    foggy idea
                              running to paradise
                    that one time
                                    standing up
                        to write that
                                  one lovely
                                          horror

        begging his publisher for a half-
        penny in his cap to pay the electrics
        in time to tune into CBC program
        about his own adopted
                        genius
                                          no, the honour i would ask
                                          has passed
                                                  pebbles   other
                                                  underfoot   graves

        with ownership often too much of a leap
        for me to make, I told the largest hare
        the one who scrutinizes
                        but does not
                                  hop
                                      away
        when you cite raw
                    Anacreon
                              (in defence of what, exactly?)
            at him   adding
                              that more of my work is filling
                              drawers than ever before & Laforgue
                              might like that conceit & other
                              things found wanting

in these lean times, a few
morsels of Heraclitus would do, maybe a few bars
of that peculiar quintet
& that Brahms story at long last
to complete this composite of mystery
loves,   enjoying
porches of ears

10

The media may be
in touch before the close
of the cruellest month
about our unburied
                    ergo, the
                    ergot that drove men mad
& made them
                see witches everywhere
another
            chapter in the archive
                        of Mass. –
            then fresh   ,
from warm
embrace, hands
        that sift the grain, eyes
                that define quality
the elevator
phased out
with offers
of retraining
                then again, against
            the grain
                    Morse, *père*,
                        "father of American
            geography,"
held the
    lectern fast
        against French
                Illuminati
                        & wasn't so keen on the skull-
                        measuring gloss on Native
                        Americans in *Encyclopædia
                        Britannica*
                            & hoped for grand
                            "civilization," blessings
                            on heathen lands
                            & happenstance
    in his *Report to the Secretary
    of War of the United States
    on Indian Affairs*:

The introduction of spiritous liquors ...

The custom, universal among the Traders, of giving a credit
to the Indians, in its operation, is injurious both to their interests

and morals. A considerable number of those who are credited
never pay. This loss, the Traders take care to make up, by an
increased charge on the goods sold to those who do pay. The
consequence is, injustice to the honest Indian, and temptation
to him to become dishonest in return

but it's all in the
family, instantly   Let the
contemporaneous   eagle
                in that long face   soar!
                                by failed
                                painter
                                        Morse, *fils*
from the moment de Mors   (assuming grandfather's
left Mörs to rally the land   crowded teeth behind
claim of William the   all that
Bastard, then   unsmilingness)
down the line, dipping quills
    in that Cromwellian
                    well
                        of distrust
        trading up failed
        tradesman for hard
        sell of Lord
                    Protection
        racket
                (severing remote umbilical from Rome
                    with Sir Thomas & a massacre thrown
                        in, no money down)

                                        on the other side, counter-
                                        attack – don't drink &
                                        shamanize
                                                & don't
                                                    take easy bribes
                                                    not even in
                                                    infested
                                                            blankets
                                        a chief
                                        saying there are more chiefs
                                        than _____
                                                (non-derogatory
                                                    non-denominational
                                                        mad lib)

        fading in the moonlight, that glimpse of fish
        under planks where that rod got stuck   the
        old boy drowned on the other side of the is-

land & her husband drowned & her sister
drowned in a pool of her own —
                              mourning, that
is what i would like to know   does one mourn
a place or do we really leave places   are they
more firmly fixed in these doomed
                              "forms"
                                        stubborn
myths
        of waiting at Earls Cove
                              for you & you & faint
resemblances of "you"
                        to proffer the vital means
        of transmission
                              leading me
back to the pier where the rod
                        would catch
                                        next to the museum
                                        where they took me
                                        aboard great-uncle's
                                        seiner
                                              (the one on
                                                the old fiver)
        thinking of that
                        seafarer
                              my mother
who got out
        at sixteen
                        when the axe
                              fell
& battled teamster
            types who dragged
                        their knuckles
        along the ground
                        (making our reunion
                                        comparing mayoral awards
                        sheer Telemachy
                                        hence, holding fast
                                        to helmish railing
                                        for my waterless
                                        odyssey
                                              in this odd-
                        ball harbour that
                                can get kinda icy or
                                        even a mite muddy)

serving all the do-gooders
who did not recognize
her
        for the scar
                on her back

or what about that time
                you drove on
                        down
haunted by
        Rilke
            & Glück
                    did it cross your mind suddenly like a
                            deer
                    running in front   how they ached
                    for Helen, having never seen her with
                    her nose in the air or wrapped in blue
                    towel
                            having only heard tell of her
something like on the drive up
as if the gods had gambled on
the towel falling to floor

                    now
                            relatively stable around
                zero
                    the window no longer freezing
            open
                    families emerge
                            for the first time
        since the drop
                    & the girls handle
        dubious snow
                    & yell at the wetness
            of it

                        walls of snow
                                melting into mud
                puddles
                                        it is clear
                        none of this
                                will hold
                                    for much longer

for Ralph Maud

Flame,
afloat through coastal mist
in Turneresque
abstraction
startled
by
tall
ships
while to the tune of *Tannhäuser*
Natives in a Paul Kane
painting stretch out
luxuriate in
that sixpenny
vacillations   pamphlet
of ennui-   touching upon
afflicted   "Ulf's thingamajig"
parties
the poet   twenty-nine and a half inches long
tormented   five inches
at the feet   at the mouth
of tightly gilded   the UK dailies   (that band
dulcet-   getting their angle   of old
voiced   of blond curator   mad
Waltraud   grasping its curve   animals)
this vague
two geese   migration
the first to return   along trade
take a sip of temporary   routes
rivulets   from the Middle
outside   East

then Northern
Wakashan   or Southern
speakers   forming
a V
when there was
an ice
recession on
(the means of transmission)

the loan of <u>The Horn
of Ulf</u> found a place

in Morse's canvas
depicting
expansion
in the
Palliser
Triangle
& beyond

barters for this (eye)
catcher *they clepe us*   releases
drunkards and with   back into wild
swinish phrase   adversarial place
soil   names
our addition

the ivory horn browning   Homer & Virgil

the jackrabbits browning   evasive about

which was the

route of "false

dreams,"   a story of ivory or horn
already plotted
in *The Romance*
of *Canadian History, Volume III: The*
Uncharted

Nations
charm
offensive   I, Aggressive Botherer of Geography
must cross-reference with what that
blessed earth informs the gut,   learns
me to like wild rice & yams, for example

YAMS DO
NOT EXIST
between either prairie

when the "huns"   *gaxseme* – "straddling
are on the run, or   on surface"
grey partridges
(*Perdix*
perdix, less loved
than Icarus
& pushed off
into trust
fall

                                                    wing-
                                                        less)

        scatter
                for atavistic scatter-
        shot
                then kick up sand
                over those Mesopotamian
                origins [calling to mind the
                strange temple on Scarth   the Gryphon
                where they dressed Louis   symbol of the Sun
                like one of the police   confronts that Chimæra
                & did justice that day   of Winter
                & put up a plaque   over the Tree
                in nearby park   of Life we & the Tlingit
                & announced a day   stitch button
                in his honour]   by button
                                    over the cloaks
Who will rid me   on our backs
of this Ulphus?

                                        tewese − "attack
                − the Date   on beach
                            Palm   or struggle
                perhaps   against ebb
                            those rays   tide"
                                        that revivify
                            the earth
        ovipositor leaving a choir
        of non-pests   the female spray-
                embedded   foam applicator
                        in the soil   happy to be one
        in lesser numbers   of few in the trade
                more likely to
                        survive
                            everyone transformed into
                                            Hungarian partridges
                        at the last second, presumably

                                            two-winged genii
        recall the Feast   on Sumerian
            of Mithras   figure,   two
                    deity of Light   white-tailed hares
                        & Air   bloated with want
vague
        these migrations
        these multiple   or maybe, flame
                routes to one's   that

getting by   *grand*

      L!ets!e – "sunlit   *tremolo*

             place"   you talk of

pouring from horn   HMS *Discovery*

upon little tree   was just setting off

outside, hampered   when I got this

by plastic refuse   might be home

reviewing Old English code   after all

& edicts against forbidden love:

ne quis adoret   this time of renewal

alicujus generis   by our calculations

arborum ligna   this time is now

12

Flames, say
the names, even this mistaken
place name

Del mio pensiero tu sei
regina
tu di mia vita sei
lo splendor

I would like to give you
back
your endless sky
sweet breezes
of your Native soil
a royal garland for your
autochthonous head
a seat of influence·
next to the sun

the Queen
bursting into room
beaten gold
as cockneys   if you just ate
cram beef-   that up you lack
eater pockets   selenium, fatty
full of Jubilee   acids, enzymes
Mix,   a lifesaver in the Yukon
let me tell you

croon me
fish bones
left by bears
to nourish the
roots
you know if I had my druthers
I would admit to my lady
Regina
is a complex
of contrarian
occasions

but today the clouds   are moving along
(*Regina   the clouds can be beautiful!*   )
they do not

                    appear in the
        slightest
                    lonely

over continual agitation
     & Köchel 516
        in consolation
for yesterday's RSO
demonstration (for restless kids?)
    the hand strain under advisement
                              & the French
                    horn
                              opening up
           like a mouthful
                    of spit
           (condensation!)

        We feel here the sort of rediscovery of possibility
        described by many who endure glimpses of the void
        beyond. The astute listener may recognize
                                        here
                    themes which seem to look
backward and borrow vocabulary
     from earlier, more troubled parts
                         of the piece

        then today, changing
        my mind & cancelling
        plans
                there is certainly no
                ode to the north wind

                              sidelong eyeing lady
                              friend of the oboist
                              restless & it was
                              mutual (longing
                                   for semi-
                                   comic sorrow
                                   of bassoon)
yet somehow, history sticks

In the second half of the nineteenth century, a cylindrical heap of buffalo
bones appeared and the mound began to grow and grow   For the longest
time, it was thought to have been the "happy hunting ground" of
First Nations and Métis hunters but the bones may have been a ghostly

admonition about the small-
pox epidemic   In other words, by no means
                should you hunt here

However, the name stuck and the area was known as Pile o' Bones, Many-
bones, Bone Creek, and more exotically, as Tas d'Os

"Oskana," the Cree word for bones, was mistakenly taken down by Captain
Palliser as "Wascana" and that name stuck too
                                        A lot of things stick here, and
perhaps that is because the city was built on soil that has been described by
our friend Edward McCourt as a gumbo clay that adheres to whatever it
touches with the tenacity of molasses   Indeed, to this day, there is
no record in the census of how many
                                boots fell victim
                                                to this unpaved muck
before roads and pavement
                        were poured
                                in

        Tas
        d'Os Pile o'
        Many Bones
        Bone Creek

                "the place where
                        the bones are"

                        unless these
                        are for export

meanwhile I have gotten my origin
story straight & in my settlement
will settle on the yellow two-
storey across the way
                that catches
                        the light
the way Vermeer
                saw Delft
        through that
                camera
                obscura
                        [according to a
                        figment of Proust]

                                        O flames
                                      say the names
dream a Xanadu of   while my face is
      xŭmdas – "land otter place"

    until something stirs   buried under the squeaky floorboards
                                 of proems
                                       & ecologically sound paeans
                                          to ethical conduct
            so long as we can sit inside
            when winter is bearing down
            waiting for "starlight tour"
            to reconnote itself, hey

along the filament from an earlier movement

the bones are stirring underfoot

each shriek between ourselves
                        & the north wind

COMPANY
ROMANCE

Summer or winter, it was a life of wild
adventure and daily romance.

— AGNES CHRISTINA LAUT
  The "Adventures of England" on Hudson Bay:
  A Chronicle of the Fur Trade in the North

for Henry Hudson, worming through   ice   floes
to prove that Empire is odyssey, perhaps
lost on a crew that was shanghaied, the
frozen glory of the New World not
exactly their cup of tea.
                         Old Juet raged with open
insolence and Henry Greene, the guttersnipe,
whispered of mutinous delights that awaited
the pluckiest of the lot (presumably in plum-
in-mouth patois) because no one would hear
a muffled cry but gull, tern, bittern, phalarope,
goose, duck, and hooting piebald loon
and they shivered for months on end
without any inkling of how warm
fur can be.
                 Apparently, this was not the way to
China, and then the equinoctial gales raised
waves over the *Discovery*, and Juet lost it,
and lost his wages, now a doleful rat
on a sinking ship, metaphorically
speaking.
                 When the gunner died, it was the
overcoat that did it, a point of hierarchy
even here, over who was entitled to it,
and they must have remembered that
summer, when the captain was handing
out the last of the bread.
                         Juet and Greene
forced the issue, and they lowered Hudson
and his son and seven loyal chaps into a
piddly boat, unknowingly marking the
starting point for a fractious trade war,
and Greene was a grim Limey gathering
sorrel grass when the Inuit nailed him,
unfailing in knowing right from wrong,
and Juet died outside of Ireland with
a curse upon his starving lips.

Legend has it that an old house
battered with bullets belonged to a cast-
away, even before the Big Company came,
and that man lived among the Natives
for untold centuries, nursing his spleen,
waiting for the day when he would call
to account the use of his name in vain.

Rupert of the Rhine in his lonely tower
mopes with much-lampooned poodle
that familiar with dark invisible arts
bored of richly liveried blackamoors
and his fashionable appendage boy
and the slave trade in West Africa
is not quite what it was.

There he broods, still bristling
over Digby's digs about Bristol
when not polluting Chelsea
with his plate-glass houses
however that iron-zinc alloy
led to lovely rounds of lead
blessing head after head
with the perfect product
brassy and beautiful as
his shattering glass tear-
                drops
                    "Rupert's
                        drops."

Hole in periwig aside
he had such a passion for
the geometry of war
though his personal cannon
put him a shade in the red
surely his autobiography
was a cracking good read
had it not gone missing.

Skiffing out from Wapping Old
                        Stairs
                            to a ketch
                            known as
                            Nonsuch
where a bottle of Madeira
                    was broached.

He had never been so happy
naming things not his own.

was no longer dancing in gilt shoes
so our émigré fiddler from Italy
went to the grand trouble of making up
French opera, the most sumptuous
propaganda for export, still ringing in
Bach's ears unfashionably late. Frogs
out of Ovid scattered in the fountain
outside as a reminder that rebellion
is futile. Versailles had arisen out of
suspect muck and much like in credit
card ads, *anything was possible*
                              while
                                      a New
France was losing ground in our
virgin home and native land and
Intendant Talon was concerned
about penetration of the North
really pretty edgy about major penetration
by those gross *anglais* led by Des Groseilliers.

What went on in the mind of Fouquet
tittering over Molière's *Les Fâcheux*
at a gathering rather too splendid
for dandies handling public coffers
before that shocking surprise bust
by d'Artagnan and the musketeers
before murmuring furtively with a
mythical man in an iron mask, did
he perhaps envision the conquest
of the *filles du roi*, often confused
with *filles de joie* exhibiting an air of
joie de vivre in Jefferys's watercolour?

There is not even a sketchy sketch
of twelve-year-old orphan girls who
wince under old lechers, only lying
back and thinking of a new colony.

At Moose River, one chief could not take
his eyes off Des Groseilliers, recognizing a
skinflint dealer that had left them skint
and challenged the Frenchman:

> "But you drove hard bargains. You took
> our silkiest, softest and richest furs, and
> you gave us but beads and ribbons. You
> told us the skins of the sable, and marten,
> and beaver were of little account to you ..."

Presumably en route to mastering the Queen's
English, Gooseberry said that they now smelt
the blood of an Englishman and the bad old
days were already far behind them and from
now on
        everything would be plum dandy.

so enterprising and vigorous, credited
with deeper white penetration, in spite
of mission dysfunction, asking for
directions from Winipek, that body
of muddy water, to the Western Sea
and the Natives saying it was nearby,
another ten days by way of a great
river that flows directly toward the
setting sun. Nab the furs and plant
the fear of God into their hearts
was his way, having the heart of a
colonizer rather than a wayfinder.

It was an exhausting slog, trying to
convert primitive peoples, and most
everyone said "no thanks" but the
Sioux said it more pointedly, coming
from a more violent land, but our
goodly godly benefactor preached
to our adorable first folks of peace,
handing out guns and ammunition
to seal the deal, only getting himself
dragged into more war with the Sioux.

Rough and ready with fine intentions
he would not shrink from cuddling
the Cree when they were close to
decimation from smallpox, and
everyone could see that it hurt
at first (white penetration!) but
love could grow in a lacrustine
basin, just like wheat or peas.

La Vérendrye died then, begging
Natives not to follow the northern
route, still dreaming of the Western
Sea, while his son, the Chevalier,
got as far as the foothills of the
Rocky Mountains, following in
his father's footsteps of not
quite knowing what is what.

Cocking was not particularly cocky
for a Company man, not accepting
cock-ups that splashed him in the
face like so many rapids, lacking
the Frenchie *savoir faire* to make
Native canoes and conduct them
no less, from point A to point B.

The inferiority complex of him
and his fellows floated ahead
wherever they bungled along
and whenever he dangled a
bauble for a pelt, and found
the French had already got
there first, he wrote in his
journal that the Natives
are lying liars full of lies.

When the winter of his dis-
content turned glorious summer
by this fort of York, Cocking
kvetched about the mosquitoes
and lack of food, and could not
understand for the life of him
why Natives kept burning his
bribes to bring about a change
in their situation, or why they
sometimes got so very upset.

With a stiff upper lip, Cocking
found the three Native ladies
that were right for him, and
likely gleaned the sun would
never set on HBC, hereinafter
called the Company, and that
one day I'd have nowhere else
to buy my g_ddamned pants.

with all the means in his power so that the C_'s enter-

prises should not fail the C_ exhorted them to devote

themselves to activities more profitable than such fruit-

less war parties   the C_ found it necessary for fear of

eventual failure the C_ was preoccupied with Canadian

penetration did the C_ succeed in imposing its tutelage

over those territories   the double plan that resulted

in the C_'s creation the C_ was concerned   the C_

did not contemplate remaining entirely immobile   in

this fragmentation of [the C_'s] forces the C_'s officers

refused to believe in the existence of horses   the C_'s

adversaries the C_ was to escape for a while   the C_

itself hampered   the C_ resumed possession   the C_

gradually turned away forbidden access to the C_'s the

C_ set out to stabilize its positions in the interior   the

C_'s tardy entry that in size rivalled the C_'s enterprises

was inspired by the idea of Protestant crusade   the C_

in fact never completely overcame its feeling of mistrust

toward the native peoples contested openly the legality

of the charter held by the C_ and the right the C_ invoked

to sole occupation of the territories the C_ does not seem

to have taken account of difficulties service in the interior

involved

blessed by her "rude upbringing"
picks berries and wild fruits
for pemmican, extracts
                    sap
from maple and birch for
our contemporary villain, sugar,
dresses bison skins, "her patience
never daunted by this laborious
and tiresome work," makes
mittens, moccasins, leggings, snow-
shoes, gloves laced and stitched with
sinews drawn from muscles of elk
and moose, slyly intercepts
customers of the Company
and their gifts of meat, gathers
pitch for waterproofing roofs,
prepares wattap needed to join sheets of
bark from which canoes are made,
skins animals and collects their by-
products needed for winter provisions,
sets up and takes down camp and
(often) drags plenty of baggage, etc.

The bourgeois simply could
not do without her, and willing
or no, she was his for a bottle of
plonk or a bundle of tobacco, but
it would be pretty swell if you
got one or even two horses.

The ████████ Company in fact never completely overcame its feeling of mistrust toward the native peoples. In any too-close contact between its employers and ████ ████████████████████████ clandestine trafficking that would have been prejudicial to its interests, ████████████████████████ to keep apart these groups whom *the hazards of life had destined to come together.* By forbidding ████████████████████████████████ ████████████████████████████ immure them in the posts and prevent their access to the "plantations" ████████████████████ the Committee ████████████████████████ to the trade. To this excessive caution, ████████████████████ Anglo-Saxon temperament ████████████████████ one must add a genuine fear of the native peoples, ████ ████ in the Company's eyes, encourage aggressive attitudes and even surprise ████

was not around to *scotch* the narrative:

landlords in imitation of the English
magnates, their reduction of tenants
(crofters) to increase the profits from
rearing sheep, but wherever to dump
diaspora of unruly rural types, pride
of one clan exchanged for another
in the New World, rapid as a dodgy
global heart transplant, no questions
asked?

    "The very security of Britain"
called for removal of such elements
only not to enrich that ghastly Yank
republic, so why not straighten them
out somewhere around the strait of
Manitou?

    Lord Selkirk came up with
a quick fix (or kludge) for the troubles
of his native land, an unbeatable deal
for the Company, graciously "ceding"
116,000 acres of land to our earl for
ten shillings, only don't spend it all
in one place!

    This foundation of the
colony of Assiniboia transformed
civil and criminal jurisdiction into
the "private law" of the Company
(and totally not the other company)
with the magic root word in a dead
language being
        "privilege."
From then on
        "passing the buck"
took on new meaning, and it was
even worse than when your cousin's
a chief and you think he's puffed up
but for my part, restitution would be
the Company selling me a discounted
belt that doesn't *scotch* so bloody fast.

Bleak, dreary, cheerless, yet throbbing
with the virility of the life of a new
country. Pioneering, trading, bartering,
that was the life
                  inside the walls
                           of old Fort
Garry. They were
men that lived there, rough-
cast, rough-
hewn, fearless, dauntless
men.
        The West was no place for weaklings
in those days. The struggle
                    cut
                      them
                          down

        timber
            laid
the foundations,   spread
later from Winnipeg
                to the last great West.

Whereas the Governor and Company of ███████████, have ceded to the Right Honourable Thomas Earl of Selkirk, his heirs and successors,

for ever,

all that tract of land or territory,

bounded by a line running as follows, viz: – Beginning on the western shore of the Lake Winnipic, at a point in fifty-two degrees and thirty minutes north latitude; and thence running due west to the Lake Winipigashish, otherwise called Little Winnipic; then in a southerly direction through the said lake, so as to strike its western shore in latitude fifty-two degrees; then due west to the place where the parallel of fifty-two degrees north latitude, intersects the western branch of Red River, otherwise called Ossiniboine River; then due south from that point of intersection to the height of land which separates the waters running into Hudson's Bay from those of the Mississouri and Mississippi Rivers; then in an easterly direction along the height of land to the source of the River Winnipic, (meaning by such last named river the principal branch of the waters which unite in the Lake Ságinagas,) thence along the main stream of those waters and the middle of the several lakes through which they pass, to the mouth of the Winnipic River; and thence in a northerly direction through the middle of the Lake Winnipic, to the place of beginning. Which territory is called Ossiniboia, and of which I, the undersigned, have been duly appointed Governor. And whereas, the welfare of the families, at present forming Settlements on the Red River, within the said Territory, with those on the way to it, passing the winter at York and Churchill Forts in Hudson's Bay; as also those who are expected to arrive next autumn; renders it a nece-sary and indispensable part of my duty to provide for their support; in the yet uncultivated state of the country, the ordinary resources derived from the buffalo and other wild animals hunted within

the Territory,

are not deemed more than adequate for the requisite supply. Wherefore, it is hereby ordered, that no persons trading in furs or provisions within the Territory, for the Honourable ███████████ Company, or the ███████████ Company,

or any individual, or unconnected traders or persons whatever, shall take out any provisions, either of flesh, fish, grain, or vegetable, procured or raised within the Territory, by water or land carriage, for one twelvemonth from the date hereof; save and except what may be judged necessary for the trading parties at this present time within the Territory, to carry them to their respective destinations; and who may, on due application to me, obtain a license for the same. The provisions procured and raised as above shall be taken for the use of the colony; and that no loss may accrue to the parties concerned, they will be paid for by British bills at the customary rates. And be it hereby further made known, that whosoever shall be detected in attempting to convey out, or shall aid and assist in carrying out, or attempting to carry out, any provisions prohibited as above, either by water or land, shall be taken into custody, and prosecuted as the laws in such cases direct; and the provisions so taken, as well as any goods and chattels, of what nature soever, which may be taken along with them, and also the craft, carriages and cattle instrumental in conveying away the same to any part, but to the Settlement on Red River, shall be

forfeited.

*The Company (the other company) could now prepare
the attack on the colony which it had contemplated.*

One slogan
might have been "The Perfect Body" with Duncan
Cameron holding auditions for his vision of the
"Imaginary Indian" in a montage with a fast beat

> *That scapegoat's gotta be found!*
> *That Indian's gotta be made up!*

life coaching mixed-blood officers, office clerks
to put feathers in their hair and paint their faces
with vermilion, trying out a cappella war song
before adding another drum solo, then asking
them to practise that pillage one more time ...

Miles Macdonell's dim view of heathen savages
did not help matters, and as governor or middle-
manager he was low on cojones, playing into the
sleight of hand of Cameron, who knew it was
all about branding. Those memos sent by non-
Natives to Natives about their fab autonomy
was nothing new under the sun that never
sets (I only got one by sext the other day).

Ersatz atavism and the spectre of random
violence had become the perfect product
of North America, the kind of open-air
theatre that was good for business, and
any accord that was reached between the
Company and the Métis was quashed by
the North Westers who demanded that
Assiniboia be destroyed on the spot.

To be continued ...

Reverend R.G. MacBeth

Out, damned spot! out, I say! ...What! will these hands ne'er be clean?
— SHAKESPEARE, *Macbeth*

It appears certain that the French half-
breeds who were settled
on the south branch of the Saskatchewan River ... were determined
to hold to the old system of
long narrow farms fronting on the river, as
against the
rectangular,
or "square,"   survey proposed by the Government, which threatened

up
to break

the homes they had built and overturn the old social life fostered by
contiguous residence; and it seems also tolerably clear that many of
the settlers had been waiting an extraordinarily long time for their
land patents and scrip. These things were sufficient to
unsettle
the easily ruffled and somewhat turbulent half-
breed element, and once anything like rebellion was
contemplated, the aid of their
duskier brethren
all over the great plains was
confidently expected.
On our side, the old 9-pounder
sending shell
screaming into the thicket
on the hill-top

Humanly speaking, I have never been able to
make out why the enemy, who were in force
outnumbering us three to one, did not make
short work of us
in the darkness.

Robert Semple, simple in some ways, and middle
management had a lot to answer for, there being
too few Indians and not enough chiefs
of the colony. Colin Robertson's attempts
at peace ran up against that herrings-and-
porridge constitution and indigestible
contempt for indigenous descendants
that churned in Semple's stomach
like butter with the scum un-
skimmed.

        Thus, the customer (of colour)
was not always right. Today, our elders
would maybe hit the fourth floor in an
emergency, passing bedding clerks full
of goss about that waning Company
love affair
        along with the dreary death
rattle of capital, long after
                fear in the
cloud enveloped
        the Métis

when muskets, pistols, daggers, bows
and swords shook under the figure-
eight logo of that "New Nation"
in this catalogue of the other company
in this fashion show of fabulous war
dress from other peoples
            but the raiding
workshops for weekend warriors went
awry the second Semple got up a posse
and charged the troupe at Seven Oaks
and it was a simple thing, to wildly
shake the bridle of his rival's horse
but somebody
        (who couldn't tell a
           famished Métis from Chief Rain-
           in-the-Face when Fetterman dis-
           obeyed orders not to "engage
           or pursue Indians" and got
           all his men massacred)
got trigger itchy
and the rest, my friends
        is history.

Paul Kane's paintings constitute
a unique, ethno/logical, albeit
romanticized record of the First
Nations
      of nineteenth-century
  North
       America
               Reflective of the European
       aesthetic of the picturesque
   the composition shows
            A
   Renaissance-inspired
  tree is used
       as a framing
 device
in the foreground;   the influences
  the artist absorbed
           by copying Old
Masters
     are readily apparent
            Although he set out
to accurately record
         a turning point
             in North American
    history, the moment before
indigenous culture was tho/roughly
              disrupted by
   colonization
     and settlement, he did so from the
colonialist
     point of view
         (of his time)
   which imposed
       romantic notions of
the idyllic, the
     exotic, and the
         "noble
 savage"
    on his
      subjects.

Go on
      go along the Loop, past the vape looks,
past the obligatory Kwakwaka'wakw totem in
tiny prairie "park" towered over by the head
of Statesman Riel, presumably brandishing
evidence that his "provisional government"
was de facto government, that his leader-
ship was as elected representative for
folks who needed food, particularly
after the Pemmican Proclamation
and corporate guidelines became
law of the land, leaving the Prime
Minister to deliberate whether
sympathetic Quebec or outraged
Ontario could hurt him more in
the polls and the wind ended up blowing
                in the direction
                    of a Regina
                      noose
relying on the usual better-you-than-me logic
but go along Esplanade Riel, past the Mid-
town Murder, past the façade of so much
G_d-fearing abuse, past the memory of One
Arrow on a treason charge, his last words
being
      "Do not mistreat my people"
                unearthed
and returned to Saskatchewan as
rebel hero, and past the fee notice
about wedding photos to find the
other
      Riel, displaced
                from across the river
for being the instrument of crazed angels
or simply grappling with mood disorder,
this quiet man led away from teaching,
riding into battle naked with more fury
than a Napoleonic complex that is funny
for such a large sculpture of metaphysical
anguish, inspired by Rodin's treatment of
suffering, yet not quite Canadian enough
or "Indian" enough (or too "Indian"!)
down to the double helix of his blood
to float up like a Chagall and shake the
perfect mercurial nudity of Golden Boy
in CTV shot to kick off Grey Cup 2015!

YOU'VE GOT A DATE
WITH A ~~BLOND~~
BOND

BUY VICTORY BONDS

— Canadian World War II Poster

If only it were that easy. Forget about settlers,
forget about status card past expiration date,
forget about the whole cash-nexus bromance,
crash the chitkicker's ball with muddy scrip,
settle down with that gal from Morse with
aegis on her breast and Bettie Page on her
biceps. The little ones would maybe pass as
Métis and cease to haunt these desecrated
cemeteries or glorious opportunities going
like IHOP pancake revolution built on the
remains of Native backs. We would take
    down
          the mezuzah
                for luck
                        if not
belief whistling in the dark while we
wring out all our filthy laundry and
fan it dry in an excellent north wind.

If only we could give up the Company,
forget about the implications of beet
sugar and the gleeful burning of books
on If Day in downtown Winnipeg
to push more Victory Bonds, or even
last night's boil-water advisory, agape
for tests to reveal that E. coli causes
racism, or lonely folks in Fargo who
prefer white sex, or big-boned babes
who insist upon big brown nobblers.

Then the gal from Morse would sit
on my knee and we would consider
economic theories that suggest a
course of excessive consumption
invariably leads to similar forms
of global macrocannibalism, from
Cree Wîhtikow to Kwakwaka'wakw
Bakbakwalanooksiwae, ravenous

eater of initiates, leeching culture,
language, and song from the poor
sap subject to certain enzymes
in his swelling belly, or how our
reformation and telegraphy got
mixed up with massacre and
slavery and how our sun will
burn up long before its evil
twin Nemesis or Andromeda-
Milky Way collision can ruin
our afternoon, or according
to a haphazard inversion
of the Fermi Paradox, we
won't make contact once
we have snuffed ourselves.

If only it were that easy. Boil
water again and iron out all the
kinks, all the Yiddishkeit until
                    we occupy that prairie long poem
rumoured to be extinct like anything
    nomadic
             or migratory, and then learn
that gal to take splendid pictures of
nothing,   say
              that
              grain
              elevator
                    in Morse

where everyone parks in the middle
stumbling over forgotten graves
with author selfie next to town sign
another stock photo of her prairie
        heart
              exhumed, suspended
in squares of
pure yellow
              maybe mustard or canola
if we knew, yes
              if we knew for sure.

> *I would trade the whole of Haida art for the Mozart horn concertos.*
> — BILL REID

Friends, had the romance of New World exploration
not hit a rocky patch, I would at the very least barter
for the complexity of the string quintets, or something
with a clarinet in it. Walking in the imaginary steps of
the Wakashan speakers, wherever I go, there I am
reclaiming caches of magic from undusted centuries
but the feds have me under surveillance, so any hint
of dissent is woven into vintage airs that befuddle
even the most fluent Italians:

> *I miei parenti*
> *sognaro un trono*
> *e li destò la scure!*
> *O quando*
> *fine avran*
> *le mie sventure ...*

You see, in the First Nations production of *The
Magic Flute*, I was kind of disappointed at that
glaring omission: the day Mozart died (stupidly
meaning likely of strep throat), Lt. Broughton's
"right hand" was shooting an Aboriginal while
still en route to a harbour of Dickensian convict
ships but history is sometimes a bitch like that
and besides, I'm out of work and off to the King's
Head to bum some soda water and celebrate the
masonic grandeur of some Secret Handshake
Society with one of Gottlieb's salient tunes
that used to kick off Manitoba legislature
seances:

> *In diesen heil'gen Mauern*
> *Wo Mensch den Menschen liebt*
> *Kann kein Verräter lauern*
> *Weil man dem Feind vergibt.*

Colonization has worked so fanfuckingtastic on
this planet, in less than a decade, in some Karel
Čapek nightmare, we are going to try our luck
on Mars, digging up whatever underwater life
we can find, and give them guns and tobacco

and (*tabernac!*) beautiful blankets from our
benevolent Company before taking our leave
leaving more space litter than I ever expected
to see in my lifetime. Tarkovsky's *Solaris*
springs to mind, that solitary image of
our sad, lonely memories set to Bach
organ tune, polluting the irradiated
ocean of another world, and in our
collective amnesia forgetting that
Verdi put mixed-race relationships
on the stage in the 1800s, roasting
bad leadership in his operas, and
somehow without Canada Council
grant capturing my tsuris.

> *Che senza nome ed esule*
> > *In odio del destino*
> > *chiedo anelando*
> > > > *Ahi misero*
> > *la morte d'incontrar*

Friends, you must forgive my pasticcio
because I have not come to this land
of opportunity, woefully *unedumacated*
as I am, to lay claim to anything that
is yours, having given up my ancestral
ways of conquest via sensuous genius
(that are so last week, if you must know)
but if there is a bit of room, to plant
my imaginary island ceded up upon a
living prairie exhibit I should like to
call "harbour" instead of home, snacking
back every atavistically delicious bison
I can lay my hands on before we come
to some accord.

> > *Wen solche Lehren nicht erfreun*
> > *verdienet nicht ein Mensch zu sein.*

Ahhhh, Herr Mozart, I think I've got it too.

The circulation of unfathomable saps,
And the yellow-blue rise of singing phosphorus!
— ARTHUR RIMBAUD

Unannounced inténtions   the sacrosanct
móney-laundering clínker-med   fascist   fanatic
láptop-frock lapidary scórecard   Líbertad-liquídity
Logorrhea linguinë fidget-wreck   corrugated tent grámmar
    grávity-whorl   tonal dróne-pipe-Atari-Never-Néver-
Land varmints   *egoíc carpetbagger*   climatology
glóry-hole séed-pump   Chippewa venison   pínup-
honey cóalhole   piscatorial fólk-art   cokehead dupe
    tofu-focal   finicky tríbune   barebones amálgam
unam   vestal académicism tacky mendacity cóal-
        barge newt   turns herself into a tool of her árt   alien
    emótion   Maximum gíst *gone grist*   altímeter
álgae uránium   bacteria eat   *brain-eating amoéba*
plant pathólogy   bargain básement   imponderability exam
evident-mycólogy   misogynist-mythology   *Calling*
Cthulhu or this place "America" is to name it after a mend-
acious stranger   "Turtle Island" is the name given this
            continent by Native A̶m̶e̶r̶i̶c̶a̶n̶s̶ based on creation
Módeling Process   De generatiónë et corruptiónë
    polyactivist lárceny's martial-consístency panópticon-
        monopoly   *upgrade emoticon to emoji in seven business*
    days
            mélting-pot-excoriating lócust-storms
doggy*style* séntences passingly lapidary moss-
clumping links a white-pánel truck spreadeagled
by contingency sonic is semantic convictions   Group-
    think *wiping goop from stick* with headline-grabbing
solitude   subtle bituminous statue supplanted
        ráin
            check
                gone chèque
                    neat phosphorescent
                            lozenge
heuristic decline misogyny blasphemy limitless-agriculture
Saskatchewan rabbity stewpot felicity level of héll   *Caged*
Rabbits May Save Iberian Lynx, insists olive-oil manufacturer
tagging someone in a híp commúnity shrug óff
impróperly-drawn-cóntract inscribed in grand ópera
            assimilating the best of the West and the East

Truth and Reconciliation and Algae Pods

Lake Winnipeg will
be a dead lake
by the time
I reach
age 13

— JAXTYNNE GUIBOCHE, age 3

Futurewise, we are in control of the transmission
and we control the horizontal and the vertical
but for now, wherever you go, there you are
ruining "your" land's most threatened lake.

It's not just hog farmers, rednecks, or Natives
who found dead frogs by the water, or even
big business. The apparent inability of each
primitive life form in this country to stir an
ounce of detergent in a cup of water will
obliterate your progeny. Going by all the   GO JETS GO!
things you pour down there and emit into
the air, to paraphrase John Fire Lame Deer,
you are deeply ashamed of the way you smell.

Only about half of the new/old *Outer Limits*
episodes offer hope for the human spirit of
shirtless himbos on Expo lands, in Yaletown
or along the seawall beside Coal Harbour.
                    A
poorly Photoshopped mind-controlling data
tower next to the "Golf Ball" reminds us of
that guy at NASA trying to extract biofuel
from algae, so eventually you could travel
to Mars without the hassle of fossils, and
terraform the sucker to further expand
your game plan of universal obliteration.

If we were writing these episodes so much
better, some bros from the Adam Beach
Film Institute would turn Lake Winnipeg
from national toilet bowl to algae pod
rocket fuel and Le Musée canadien pour
les droits de la personne would be our
effing mothership, proving that those
residential school tests for ESP were
spot-on, and we are going home, and
we can shape your vision to anything
our imagination can conceive ...

a friend of mine, lovely to be-
hold for being decently real
reminding of my mother or her
sister who could not hold on
or that friend who could not ever
quite get Cree vowelling down
on the verge of making a few
changes when out of nowhere
the axe
      fell.
             No elder or pooh-
bah, therefore
                MISSING
from political photo-
ops, even stock photo catalogues
and certainly never the protagonist
in novels or romantic comedies
celebrated as the "Strangler" for
not handling the Batoche bell
with enough holy holy holy
reverence
          landing in Regina
with her last few bucks, with
child without a father
                 and years
later when the young woman
went missing, the local sex
workers helped search for her
but the police did not
              though Native
folks go missing on snowy evenings
all the time
          and sketchers modify
features to sell dying newspapers
because only the perception of a
victim can reach a demographic
but whether dead or vanishing
in the age of mechanical repo-
traction
          the living are somehow
 missing
          from our syrupy hockey-
rioting six-packing cultural *whoop*
still not finding quite the right role
in our red-hot company romance.

PRAIRIE
HARBOUR
13 – 24

Nothing on either prairie changes though the winds blow
across immensities your heart would shrivel to imagine
knowing they pass between the worlds and can be heard
to do so ...

— ELI MANDEL

Flame,   rising
out of plant ashes
soaked in wet pot
tons of that thriving
fertilizer

tell spring
did not need us
very badly
I Have Slipped Away from
This World
on the verge

of Maestro Sawa's
RSO retirement
next to tattoo convention where
rows of folks from Conexus/Mosaic
clear out
before the second part of Mahler's Fifth
begins
alone
stands
French
hornist
with erotic
fist ready
(*Kräftig, nicht zu schnell*)
this Scherzo
with the tail
of a comet, thoroughly
kneaded
so that not even one grain
remains
unmixed
or unchanged
since I always insist that
nothing must be repeated —
everything has to
develop
organically
the way this initially fey
Waltz in B-flat Major
bombs
less than bounds countrified
Ländler

this charming peasant
          synthesis
& contrast
not so unlike boreal
     chorus
          frog
               under bridge
                                             many a night
               when a lonesome
               mallard interjects
                                   with soft
                                   quacks
          until countertenor killdeer
          throws them right off
          along temporary slough,   fading

     sun on the flag of a high mast
     sails after the week in port into a
     seeled fog of sunset east having come west
     going home. *typee* **tattoo the water woven as**
     the surgeon operated on another wound offhand saw
     the mentula tattooed SWAN remarked later with the
     sailor's recovery how charming how apt and the
     buoy confused exclaimed SWAN? that was SASKATCHEWAN

               Saskatchewan, you must know
               thyself very well
                                   to duck out
before the warning
horn, a sound
straight out of
          Götterdämmerung
                                   when grassland
                         birdsong turns eerie
                         chirping
                                        eighth
                              notes
               those thrillingly
               shrill

                         wood-
                    winds
                              Faster Kronos!
                              Resume that rattling trot!
                              Briskly bumps along
                              Over stick & stone that trot
                              Hurried into life!

now remember that sense of Munch's
painting at MoMA, that lady
with red locks
        & no ghoul to
           dance with
for there is little
time
    even for that famous love
         letter
    without words
        the Adagietto
             that stuck in the
             craw of Strauss
for the woman who (Fourth
   Symphony aside) said
        For that kind of thing
        I prefer Haydn!
he tells her everything   soulful strings
  in tones   & harp (flame!) with deepest
    & sounds   emotion, with warmth
     I feel ashamed
   of my obscenity when Gustav's
    listening –
Nowhere
    is the mood
      assisted by sung word
If the symphony did not
      begin with the slow movement – everything
  would be apparently
      in the best
        classical order
   Is one happier with a frivolous
 & unscrupulous life, or when one has
woven oneself such a beautiful and sublime
conception of the world?
        Freer in the first case – happier???
  surely not the painted knight
  from frieze
    lying in a pool
      of hemorrhage, surely not
         murky shadows
    of Klimt
      & his dearest Almschi
        over coffee
    creeping   into
     pizzicato

                    restatement
                    of over-
                    weening
                    affection
curious, as one might be at the
power of daily pettiness
that of the gifted conductor
    of his own operas
                        (even the
        future Führer clapped, seal-
like)
            Wagner might have jotted
            down (and did)
                in *Das Judentum in der Musik*:

        "the Jew can only after-speak and after-
            patch — not truly make a poem of his
                words or an artwork of his doings"

    so please forgive another slap-   the red-
    dash after-patch, packed with   winged black-
    enough haphazard claptrap   bird pursues
    to brush aside the height   a disinterested
    of fashion at the time   female
    talking of thinly veiled   then resumes
    anti-Semitism in   song on
                    Fin-de-siècle   cattails
                        Vienna   on evaporating slough
but we believe, however
that the unknowing members
    of the opposition
    of today, if they lived
one hundred years ago, would have
                    also hissed
            at Haydn   *read through his letter first*
        thing this morning
                suddenly felt warm all over. How
                    would it be if, out of love for him,
                        I were to give up —
    over blaring horn, mad   *that which has been!*
        clappers at the back
        & all that hectic
        rustic
            tension   chaos
    Apparently. The more precisely   out of which

Mahler captures outwardly the classical   a world keeps
form, the — we do not continue   being
this sentence ... Not least, a work   born
        like this symphony carries
           uneasiness in the soul   (?)
   of the critic. A mysterious Something
rules behind these unusual tone
          formations   only to fall a-
             part again at once
          primeval sounds   this
        rushing, roaring, raging sea   these
       breathtaking   scintillating   flashing
   waves

14

Flame   in this dry
                 heat the wind harbingers
                             when illicit cravings
dry out in storm
            drain
                    excited
                          by perceived
                                      crepitation
                          <that snap
                                 under fore-
               wing
                       striking vein
                             of hind-
                       wing
even this parodos chorus
for subfamily Oedipodinae
divided into two classes
(pest and non-pest)
on the basis of
                "economic
                  importance"
                                though farming first
                                gave 'em a taste
                                of something
                                beyond biome
                                greenery
            so why don't you try
            forsaking corn syrup
            for a moist meadow
            & see how you like it

I find I incorporate gneiss and coal and long-threaded moss and
      fruits and grains and esculent roots,
And am stucco'd with quadrupeds and birds all over,
And have distanced what is behind me for good reasons,
And call anything close again when I desire it

                              & then
                                    in a flash
                          out of sheer
                                    ordinariness, that bright
                                          crackling
                                          wing
                          confirmed by
            Lethbridge
            cognoscente

as *Arphia conspersa*
of the speckle-
winged
ones

on these long days beyond sultry, more
convection oven   where desire bakes in the
        broken   ground as we swear off refined
anything, less aswagger in the wake of
        those almost hobbled
                    with want

        even this stasimon chorus
        or pesticide advisory sign:

            Mosquito Control
            biorational control
            suspension concentrate
            aqueous suspension formulation
            of *Bacillus thuringiensis* sub-
            species *israelensis* strain
            AM65-52

            Mosquito Control
            biological larvicide
            is perfectly safe
            in low discharge
            bodies of wet
            with a potency
            of 1200 Inter-
            national Toxin Units
            per milligram against
            Aedes aegypti
            larvae

flame   that is faint apparition of Eros
(something Socrates maybe got wind of)
touched upon
                then lost to addlepated
        idyll
                [stock image
                of family smiling
                in CCF sun-
                        shine]
with no murmur on the night
element or amorphous shapes
it assumes

                or fleeting meeting in ice
house
                hand in hand
                            falling upon bran
                                new cotton
                                    sacks
            while the chorale of boreal
            frogs that represent society
            are singing for themselves

    or in the view of robin
                        outside the mall
        along Lockwood Road
        pulls up
                long worms
        covetous
            of pale
                yellow
            butterflies
                            or red-
                            winged black-
                            bird enraged
                                    chasing off
                            Brewer's
                                blackbird,   that's
                one way of
                    looking at it

not telling him it was a poem I was interested in, aware I'd scare him
off, *muthologos* has lost such ground since Pindar

                                        forgetful, you see
                        (with desire)
                                        persons
                    & personal happen-
                        stance
                                lost to teeth
                                        necklaces
                        expressions such as
            "tell it
                by mouth"
                        until she got tired
                        & I had to pick up
                        the book
                                for myself
therein being at the root
                        of musical outgrowth
    involves kissin'
                cousin

missing from
       tree:

Professor Morse tells
            how he watched some of them (*Circotettix*
***verruculatus*) on Mount Washington sunning themselves, occasionally**
       the hinder part of the body
elevating   **& rapidly moving the hind**
      thighs up and down against
             the wing covers
       "producing a distinct
       'scritching' sound
           clearly audible
at a distance of three or four feet
           This act was repeated
     several times at intervals
         of a few seconds."

    & all those words
went down the wrong
    hole
       without a single
       caress from kid-
        glove
          then could I impart such
          nonsensical nothings, I
          would make a killing
now do not be alarmed,   this is   SAVE
only an isolated   BC
     shower   WOLVES!
         but the mother
rushes by,   her child (of five?)   (VOWELS?)
    with head wrapped
    in canvas roof
       of his Louis XIV
          conveyance

             & the crane
             has come down

             & the perplex
             has sprung up

             & the beavers
             (or muskrats)

             have moved on

15

Flame,   this breath
                              this brevity
your name not even on record
self-censure is the source
                         of my tepid exile
& rumours
           of uniform
                 buttocks
                        on a hot day
flouncing around Wascana   (Creek/Lake/
                 Slough)
have about as much to do with me
                 as cheerleaders in need of
                                    "sensitivity
                                    training"
but I would not soften the sentence
or stop wailing into the wee hours
when the fetish of my model headdress
shall moult no feather
                        or would they shun you
for the slightest consolation
                            like the lady struck
by lightning who reads others like little books
or the lady who deals in tea tree oil & echinacea
or the lady who emulates shamanic grandeur
or the lady who turned me into chorus frog
or the lady who dreamed of fake marble
kitchen countertop surrounding me
hurt, hoisted by her own pointed heels
after a vision about them for months
wearing gumboots in chi-chi hotels
so let the powers that be
handle me how they will
because I accept handfuls
of suffering doused in
erratic
      upbeatness
                  the wick lit rather naively
by solar heat
over grass-
hoppers
           with their own rendition of Brahms's
                                    Frei
                        aber
                              einsam

because those who have perished at sea
in war or in fire or by mournful accident
will not indulge in such music again
but if all goes relatively well, when the
"grasshopper" shall no longer be a burden
meaning the kosher metaphor of thigh or
hip or bone of the pelvis that becomes
                                        sharp &
                                prominent
after a number of years have passed
when it "feels like" minus nine
                                for an object
for which
the doctor has championed more calcium
shattered on an icy
                        parking lot,   such is my
lot
    while lyrical birds this four in the morning

    [even chipping sparrow trill
                                chipping away
                    like French historian gone demotic
                    on the Dene
                                chipping away
                    at Fort Chipewyan]

are surprised by the Dakota Sioux (or
"Poets") being incited to attack the Cree
because history is such a murky business
you must love me secretly
                            in spite of tiring of my
logorrhea, already guessing that my letter is more
conceptual than expressionist in tone
                                    its tenor
apes the voyageur, that early Company man
who rowed upstream with his goods
        much as I tremble in
                        migratory
                            leap
to face you as if the resilin had just
kicked in, restoring strength
                                yes, going the wrong way
giving up on the "Western Sea"
takes leadership & I would run for the Saskatchewan
Party if that wouldn't render me a traitor to Nation
but it comes out wrong again
forgive me for this
                    much as I forgive you

for letting me
        down
                gently enough, so softly in fact
recollection escapes me (like that third instar
between moults?)
               sorry, again, sorry
                       quid tibi
                          cum regina
is a fancy question in the ablative
that also eludes me on days
when it "feels like" either forty
above or
       below
           when even psychical reasons
feel like more or less than they actually are
recall places that reanimate past sorrows
       or people who trail along like umbilicals
              or trails of snail mail no one sends
so now that I'm out of the happening
picture (or at least lurking behind it)
wring out all that chagrin & enmity
& conjure up something less petty

      Finally – "you
      don't understand
      you're like
      a sleeping frog."

Meanwhile, I'll waste away brashly
               by the songs of the Slough

                    Flame
                       in the brain
aflutter
        with teeming
              thoughts,   notes

part of the summer chorus, but their songs are not so well known
cast into metal wind vanes, or adopted as a colophon
& an ancient Greek emblem denotes that they
                       sprang
                           from the soil
      boasting indigeneity, Athenian women
      would wear golden grasshoppers
     in their
          locks
            & everybody else was no better
than a Scythian
over the cups
          but the gloss does not really hold up
          & they were gleaming gilt cicadas
          & the term was "autochthonous"
marvellous
        unless you were a migrant
                 worker
      or struggling with First
      World problems in a
      work by Euripides:

        Proud of their rites
        Are your Saskatchewanians, natives of the land
        Not drawn from unfamiliar lineage: I to them
        Shall come unwelcome, in two points
        Defective –
        My father not a native, & myself
        Of mirthful birth

     then burst of chirp by flutter, very rapid
        small-
           amplitude movements
                    of one or both of the nearly
       horizontal
hind
    femora, whirring
           or soundless

                                        caricature of hyper-
                                        modern conductor
                                        overseeing his
                                                    Symphonie
                                                    diabolica

poking at Mahler of course
with stereotypical gesticulations
according to Glenn Gould
                    " a   scuttling "
                            nasty   upward-
                                    man
            with unbearably tense
                        dominant
                        function
                            holding
                                    down
                    "horror fanfare"

        in your broad arms
        yes, in your broad arms
                murmuring Urlicht
after Ferrier
                before placing aside
                        "primitive music
                        with all the
                        mod cons"
                                        no
                    less besotted with our
                    semitonal adjacencies
                oscillations
                kept between
                        chromatic
                        neighbours
gesticulating madly for
the bus for admonition
from driver
                as if they stop every single time
                                        when lingering
                with snatches of Erwartung
                unsteady upon tongue
                                    the senses sped
                                    on with spiritual
                                    excitement stretched
                                    out to almost painful length
                                    over faintest apparition
        unless that was just a tree
        trunk or dark jogger

& not a body
                still as this nocturnal
                        second

I know that I can bore or frighten myself rather easily by think-
ing, "I am inside; I must get out" – and have felt what the
Ancients called PANIC, i.e., been outside and felt an irrational
necessity for being indoors, for going home ...

                        in the modern sense
                        "polymorphously
                        perverse"

not the dropout
                "the laziest student in the
                Conservatoire"
                        & not the first French post-
                        Wagnerian to write a sarabande,   mind
        Satie
                purging
                        genius music
                of our
                        desire

lonely as a living sky
                afloat in
                        Nuages
                                amid abstract
                impressions
                                fluctuating   colours

        unless substrate struck
        unless chitinous sound
        recalls faint drumming
                                distant thunder
in the timpani
                then that grand wonder of
                                hypostatized
                        English
                        horn

                                but the last time
        I felt that way I took out my notebook and recorded the fact
        Soon, I was writing about the general scene, about particular
        objects that caught my attention, and the terror left me

17

To subsist
the mind
must temper
such a flame
must slough
hard, congealed
re/collections
neuronal
notions
OUT TO
LUNCH
observe that
striking
Chortophaga
viridifasciata
nymph
clinging
upside-
down
to blade
of grass
caressing with sensilla
what is new
what was new

You think my gait "spasmodic." I am in danger, Sir.
You think me "uncontrolled." I have no Tribunal ....
The Sailor cannot see the North, but knows the Needle can.

however, this afternoon
bolstered by
capability
of negative
ions
caught in a good wind
on a hillock
full of Happy
Water from BC
while the little boy
wants to freak out the ducks
but the little girl
WANTS TO
GO HOME

while
rasp of grasshopper
sparrow
rouses sub-
divisions
of hippocampus
sleepy seahorse
of re/contextualization

today, the working theory
that the "Chinese" own
all these condos devoid
of entities that not-
withstanding
will sink into
muck   up
from whence they sprang

schismatic   mentality
distinct   vulnerability
breaking   into   dashes
& dots

The subject of Indian policy, in subtle ways, involved issues
important to Morse personally. In Morse's mind, Indian society
was nonacquisitive, agrarian, and ~~patriarchal~~. It was also clear
to him that modern capitalist society, represented by the "Indian
trader," was in the process of destroying Indian society. For a
man caught between an agrarian past and a capitalist present, the
dilemma of the Indians was naturally affecting

excellent fellows of eras
long gone theorize that the
nymphs produce the adult
pheromoan [sic]
to lure the male
forming neural template
of his courtship pattern

yet the art of in-   { green nymphs
visibility can in-   flock, flutter
volve irregular dis-   toward
ruptions that help   green T-
to remain hidden   shirt made
& such multiplicity   by pretty little
of stimulation   things

                              keeps 'em local   in Zhengzhou
              decreases   your phone
              chances   made by
                        of hybridization   suicidal
                        with sympatric   drone }
                              species
                                           or variations
                                           on
Wä, lā laē
          (close enough to Rhine-
                  maiden warning of
                        dying river)
                              â la pâlēda
                                    wālatsema
            Well, then it is said
                        hella hungry
                              was the great tribe
              when Vancouver
                        came round the bend
                                           there was a gloomy
                                           mutinous air,
                                                      wafting
                                    off the missing
                                    men, formerly
                                    under Bligh
that even Strauss's *Tod*
        und Verklärung
cannot smooth out
                  but the current government
                  in this climate will not send
                  me post-
                        haste
                              to L'Anse aux Meadows
                              to verify a bit of peat

                                    for your shoulder branches
                                    are where blackbirds alight
            but the reply was rather staticky

                                    That is not to happen
                                    if I have any say in the matter –
                                    you dissociated yourself from the
                                    arrangements between us
                                    in the one way that meant
                                    you could have no hope of *that*

              handing sagas of troublesome
              poets to heads of state still
              quite Clintonesque

A function in the aetiology is suggested by the role that such agonists have in precipitating mania. It has been postulated that similar abnormalities are involved in the hyperactivity associated with the severe stages of mania

I know – there is
evidence
    Morse
persons,
by carbon date
crept ashore
here   Had built
eightplexes, had honed
sharpened implements
to attack a Blackfoot
in the back

jackrabbits
near London
Drugs on junk-
ridden patch of
Rupert's Land, then   THE
WORLD IS YOURS
biodiversity in
trompe l'oeil
pose, seldom
ever seen
    by folks in
    Urban Barn

in honour of our
conflicted Odysseus
figure
    Gabriel Dumont

Duck Lake for
a proud duck
a puddle that
makes other
mallards
    jealous

to show the Cree
that I was the best
that they should
respect me

Furthermore, the Indian "problem" involved
the conflict of independence and dependence,
autonomy and slavery. Morse, like many other
Americans, believed that the Indians were one
emblem of autonomy and independence, but
that the advance of modern white culture threat-
ened them with slavery and abject dependence

    each metaphor for the world
that is a symphony
    of discordant
thrusts
    for often the rotten
    is wrought &
    begot in slick
    succession
    out of the moist muck
(terrifying Parks Canada Heritage Site employees)
    draws
    bog iron
(forges emancipation

to scatter storytelling
grants out of the paws
of Viking interpreters)

        about the size of ship's
        iron Pitt offered for a
        Tahitian woman, then
          the lasher lashed
          by Vancouver for one
        of many transgressions

**Morse could easily have turned to any number
of issues that would have cost him less money
and energy. It is possible to speculate that the
Reverend Morse took up the Indian cause be-
cause the subject touched deeply rooted issues
in his own psyche**

flame,   cutting loose   from armed tender   *Chatham*

                    for Morse – Morse are
ho lēla gāxen,   cutting it fine but nearly
      gōkulōt   early Greeks. Morse are
Listen to me   Kelts. Morse are
      my ilk   Rus (Russia)
    that I begin to ink   banning your
this this kind of this   lace panties
         my   presently
                nâʻqēk   Morse are
           this mind   all but Chinese
           near me   labourers
           visible   assembling our
                   twitching
                      gadgetalia
          for righteous posting
          about our deeply felt
          ~~emoticons~~ (emojis)
                or

      ● ● ● — — — ● ● ●

                leaping
pulling one-   from
self together
for greeter   factory
    greeting   window
              on a propaganda
                 break

18

Flame solar head-
ache lime-green
peppery *Melanoplus*
packardii   move
protoplasm   move
; * begin asm *   mov, ax, bx
tragopogon dubius:

knee of dyed red
ambiguous *Risveglio*
della farfalla metallica
futurism without litter
e.g.,   cut grass   torn
leaf on ground   the
stink somewhere of
Mania™ *seduces un-*
leashes the inner being
of a woman   thrum
aesthetics/reserve
disruption/slices
loop tragopogon dubius

the woman drives
in circles all frickin'
day two-striped in-
stars down noxious
weed fatal to
cattle concerti draw
hares   fledgling
birds like parents
rocking to baroque
Bartoli castrato Ba-
rack cuts into BBQ
meat lineup breast-
feeding pictures on
sidebar flicker junk
shots of slough
pretty dried out
cap of wet silk
prick of ivory
tapped out   be-
guiled by rust-
coloured pronotum
chipping sparrow
at three something

in the morning
Trrrrr Trrrrr
orchestral suites
Klemperer's tell-
all under super
moon these odd
strolls through
Antonioni green-

      space   'scapes

harsh faces over water-
logged relics   "cheese"
    dice Lei   "for every
          use of modernity"
painted pines beside
mesquines pelouses
fir bird cherry
these survivors
whips of wild barley
given appointment
cascades of rhubarb
subaltern creaks
with erotic ideals
wind instrument
      projects
      tongue
      at pear
trim trim whack
gated eightplex
wash wash dirty
windows with
ACCEPTABLE
VOLUME: RED
ZONE shelver
talking to self
leaves rustle
in cinematic
eerie hiatus
    a sleep   dread
        silence   letters
that do not arrive in time
viole d'amour

Somebody != frog
put out for bog
long musical dashes
lost to plane
roar this rattle sorry
i saw the faded negative
that said you were dead
radio truck influences
cloud of dust kochia
arisen from cartoon
tumbleweed intensive
study of welling up
for alien creatures
like that hugging
machine promise
of parthenogenesis
then cannibalism
then colonization
sisters for them-
selves in bush

crickets

not so much in these
phylogenetic spermatophores
Avanguardie di desiderî
umani
uploading updates ...
cette quéquette magnifique
preps
pokes
feria
roused out of Kovalyov's
"cavatina"
Brr Brr Brr Brr Brr ...
Nos!   Nos!

; * exit   *   mov ah, 4ch
; * sheepishly *   mov al, 00
int 21h

19

Flame
           blaze anew
please heed:
              this propulsive theme
     these plagal
     cadences
                    or is game not worth candle-
        fish
            (or hooligans
        in chinook)
                game
              not really game
                             once senses
                   deter-
                        ior-
                   ate

                UNCORRECTED
tucked away in ~~uncorrupted~~
                    appendix

    or a forgotten Socrates or Aristotle before the destruction
    of the library of Alexandria (as note derisively by Berad Shaw)
    by fire in which the poes of Sappho were lost

or would you
            find a window
                      for quartet
                           as "romantic poem"
        & tack it to syllabus
            for high register
                      of violin
                         imploring over   .
                                pizzicati
            of the other
                      strings
                      Tied to no mongrel laws or flattery's page
                      No zeal have they for wrong or party rage
                      curled up
                            in window
                                  carried, as
                                  Martynov notes
                      into "sphere of
                                  lyrical
                                     contemplation"

going off
   hands in pockets, picturing
     Ma Bohème
         talking of Trudeau
           farewell
                 a
                 young woman
                 in Japan was
                 just arrested
                 for making
                 a kayak in
                 the shape
                 of her *hoo*
                     hoo { since Urban
                             Dictionary says
                             all the other
                             words are ugly }
or get thee to punnery
with the Wife of Bath
          What aileth you to grouche thus and groan
          Is it for ye would have my queynte alone?
     or let lips do
     what hands do
     in Mad Libs
     from mad-
     house
          Childern are fond of sucking sugar-candy
          And maids of sausages — larger the better
          Shopmen are fond of good sigars and brandy
          And I of blunt — and if you change the letter
          To C or K it would be quite as handy
turfed out before
tenure for suggestion
that during fur trade
"romance"
       il est né
       le divin Chapeau
beaver
     dealers & bewildered
     company men could have
     taken their marketing plan
     to the next level
     with such a swank
          canoe
              over-
         turned
           in the name of

Matthew Cocking
burning all my things
hoping that will deal
me a better hand
for this urgency
POET, ETC.
WILL WORK ~~GLADLY~~
FOR COLONIAL
APPARATUS
THINKY STUFF
DERIVATIVE MOSTLY
JUST AROUND THE
CORNER FROM
CASH
NEXUS
suddenly (!)
finding
fortune
in gluteal
cleft

you will meet
someone soon

guessing that the girl
who sells tickets
for the opera
(or films!)
at the public
library
has taken
down
the O-mouthed poster
of *Jane Eyre*
for *Nymphomaniac*
(Volumes
I & II)

likely less relevant
than its showing
Jia Zhangke's
A Touch of Sin
or Claire Denis's
Bastards
with audience still
squirming from
Faulknerian corn-
cob in complicit
voyeurism of
global capital

                    moves more
        like Monica Vitti
                through *Il deserto rosso*
                            dreaming of paradisiacal pink
                                            sand
                        before the voices
                        break through
                        & CONFUSION
                        sets in
                                    a return to clear-headedness
                                    explaining the normalcy
                                    of poisonous yellow
                                    gas fumes to her son
but this time the waltz
        with a hint of Glinka
is by no means
                    Viennese
more faint
            echo
                        of Bach's Second Partita
                        for Solo
                                Violin
        but have I not failed
my betters
opting out of post-
colonial
        minima
                cum
laude   to rave
        to chew spleen   in dusty road
                    on weedy sidewalk
            & culturally
                    spew
                                this slap-
                    dash mish-
                            mash
                                    all that has been devoured
                                    for mere centuries
                                    merely to admit
            yes, I have failed
        better
                    claiming booby
                    prize for race
                    to bottom

                    in desperation
                    on such a hot

afternoon

mining my
own quarry
for etched
metallurgy

Braziers pouring in spurts of frost — Ecstasy! — fires
in rain of wind of diamonds tossed up by terrestrial
heart eternally carbonized for us —
                                    O world! —
          Far from forgotten nooks
                                    & old flames
                    that are heard
                    that are felt

          too skint to clack up
          fitting Roman elegy
          let alone sacred
          chant
                    love, my lovely
                    love, my lovely bitch
                    when the sun is hottest

                    if you want, let us
                    while away the heat

                    (not to knock
                                    & knock
                    or play
                                    message tag)

          stay
               inside & dress-
          rehearse every act
          at least nine scenes
          without intermission

          if you want, say the
          word — you will find
          me on my back
          full of brunch, a

          new hunger eating
          through everything

20

Flame
full of idyllic
sEnTiMenTalisM
for nature's bounty
would a simple tune
suffice, say an old-timey
folk dance or
some march-like "mass
songs" set to
agitprop
shoulder to shoulder,   the
radical Marxist avant-
garde (not to be confused with Avant-
Garde Beauty Training Specialists)
gains
control over all things
music
in tune
with the first
Five Year Plan

MOWER
The foolhardy ~~ploughman~~ I well could endure,
His praise was worth nothing, his censure was poor;
Fame bade me go on and I toiled the day long,
Till the fields where he lived should be known in my song
but only the Fool
can talk truth in
quivering
quixotics
& Clare
finds his most biting
satire in the asylum
yes, but ... yes, but when one is diagnosed, but hmm ...
one is keen
to
wonder at the sane world
in prairie city quadrants
where a single patch of
WilDneSs must be ob-
literated for a few more
BIG
BOX
stores with near

                              nothing inside
                                        before this empty reflection
                                                        of an age
            to lie down in front
                              of the blades
                                                        alone, without
                              slow claps
                                                  cheers, fellow
                              feeling
like a man somewhere in Pense
SK, scratching head, guessing   *(je pense)*
that all those plants & critters
karmically don't add up to one
flooded
            basement
                        only food for grassland song-
                        birds outside Grasslands mall
                        less sexy than whales or baby
                        seals
                                  grasshopper pests feeding
                        on an authentic prairie field, or
                        an excellent simulation, pests
                        that consume noxious weeds
                        that terrify these elevated bros
                        trailing rip-roaring mufflers

                  **How to make your truck sound
                        beastly for $30!**

                  but over $40 mil for *Sunflowers*
                  still "mated" by *Irises* & the
                  Portrait of Dr. Gachet
                                        nor would Russian
                                        thistle grasshopper
                                        fare better
after pre-Gorby perestroika
      liquidates ASM
                  & RAPM
                        offering freedom
                                    from cHaOs
                        & obscurantism
      including state
      patronage for
      works
            subject to comradely peer
            review by the *pokazï*

                              (near-rhymes with?)
            for eventual publication
            (provided you behave)
                              then it was academic
                              cracking down on text-
                              less music
                                          sifted for
                              ideological
                                          semi-
                              otics
imagine the optics for a room full of others
discussing the constraint, why we can't write
about such & such on the basis of such &
such
            while the low-
                  paid pianist finds his place
                  in a cold silent
                  movie theatre
                              acquiring quite the taste
                              for satirical intrusion

                              of "low" genres
                                    & quasi-
                                    cinematic
                                                "cuts"

                  resides in the "house
                  of rest & creativity"
                  composes Second String
                  Quartet (oddly not fanfare
                  for mutual massacre
                  between Soviet forces
                        & Nazi Germany)
                                    in robust Overture
                                    for some reason, the second
                                    subject is uncertain
                                                & nervous
                                    [shrill, almost
                                       screaming would
                                       be too strong]
The Honest And True My Example Shall Be
For While A ~~Man's~~ Honest ~~His~~ Conscience Is Free
            Subject's   Its
                        sometimes we
                              imagine a violent
                                          pounding at the door
                        just like the paranoid man on the library

                    computer has no reason to be paranoid
             (right?) & is reassured repeatedly
but the radical proletarianists (RAPMists) have a point –
who wants to beat their brains about for an opera about
somebody finding a nose in a loaf of
                              Cobs bread, then try telling the
                              falsettist police about exactly
                              how it got there
(on a personal note, we've got nothing
to worry about except abandonment
on a snowy night – *imagine calling*
the cops on the cops as a percussive line
in your critically acclaimed libretto)

        Utopia, the title of a book by Sir (Saint) Thomas More (1516
        in Latin, 1551 in English), was formed in wordplay, which most
        discussions of it fail to point out. It fuses
                              two Greek prefixes,
                  ou: not, and *eu*: good; thus,
        the good place
        that is no place.   *Eutopia* is
        mentioned in the 1516 preface; and
        Sidney, in his *Apologie for Poetry* (1580),
        mentions "Sir Thomas More's Eutopia."
                                        homophonous
                        with
                    Ew!
                    offset by a cavatina
                    of grunts & gargles
                        (Molson existentialist
                        belches in the nationally
                        censored version)
        not yet an official position
until RAPM is removed, until
        Stalin
            & his retinue
                    lumber out of *The Lady*
                    Macbeth of the Mtsensk
                    District
                        an exposé of emotional
                        "life" in an inhuman
                                        world
subject to unsigned editorial in *Pravda*:

"Left deviationism in opera
grows out of the same source as
left deviationism in painting,
in poetry, in pedagogy, in
                    science"

                              meeting Social Realism's
                              demands that art be
                              rooted in folklore or
                              styles familiar
                              & meaningful
                                        TO ALL
                              without special
                              preparation
but that has nothing to do with the
proud prairie tradition of removing
trees or levelling the playing field
                    branches of rare order,
                    observable in Tragopogon or Goats-beard, conformable
                    to the Spider's web, and the Radii in like manner telarely inter-
                    woven
absorbing all things
    quincuncially, muddling through
            morphemes of Recitative & Romance
                    to find voices from
                        suppressed operas
                                    speaking (?) in the first violin
                                        with sackcloth over its head
amid "Jewish" inflections
    that saturate the
                        usual tsuris
                            with their syncopated
            rhythms, principally
            aesthetic
                    but also perhaps
                    in opposition
                            to increasing anti-
                            Semitism within
                            the USSR
                                    however a mood
                                disorder can lead
                            to mAnIc
                    anger out of
                            nowhere
                but if the doctor
                in Walmart clinic

prescribes
        the "right" drug
in conjunction
        with anxiety
        checklist
then the very real voices
  .   This reformist yet
                        "bourgeois" conception is rejected
    with increasing vehemence and contempt by those who are
    disillusioned with politics and for whom art has become a
        superior form of existence with no utilitarian
                                        application
may fade, sink into
depressions in the field
over loss of its singular
stupid untamed beauty
or even the diverse
colours of sleeve-
        tugging
                acquaintances *Melanoplus*
                    sanguinipes
                        & bivittatus
                                in lieu of Morse's
                                more exotic find
                    Melanoplus
                    deceptus
only a spring home for hiding
                    hares
    Through well-known beaten paths each nimbling hare
    Sturts quick as fear, and seeks its hidden lair

        on the square
        sliced into mean
        squares of lawn

        square where
        all is in order
        wood & flower
where "maudits"
        begin to scandalize the middle
            classes by their appearance, their morals, their aesthetics
            and their despair. Many more visionary outcasts will
            later follow the anti-social path, compensating for their

sense of exile
              by an increasingly "occult" view of poetic
        creativity as magical operation

                                        or fast, restless
                                    dark, brooding
                                  even menacing
                                            mechanized
                                  waltz

                    with each of the four
                    instruments relatively muted
        save for agitation
        leading toward *attacca*
                              no, the green of
                        another Dollarama
                                    is just what
                        the area needs
                                you know, for that sense of
                                community interactivity
                                in the online simulation
                                of that Fontaine Bleu
                                Dream Machine
        but the day the noon-
        flowers are ~~mowed~~
        down   MURDERED(?)
        I drop words like "environ-
        mental
                reserve" & "bio-
        diversity"
                      from my vocabulary
                        yes my vocabulary
                              my vocabulary
                                    did this to me
              stuck for a split
              second
                        in ostinato rut
                                    winding down
                                    after klezmer
                                            "oom-pa"
                                in the cello
        before theme
                          & variations
        becomes
                    fragmented
                              the pace
        slowing with parody

of a *maggiore*
                    variation

·

        NO
            that sudden flash
of colour
            that scratch of toothy ·
                leg against leathery
    tegmina
                in that type a sound almost like

                                                scoffing
sorry, my mistake, must
be another episode
                in the brilliant
            recapitulation
over little
        more than

            a   dead   field

21

Flame
"for whom I
shelter profound
professional respect
& tender
personal
feelings"
this morning amid incessant
pffffffft
of the male black-
winged grasshoppers
("scoff/laws" [*sic*])
a female
bent her antennae
down, presumably
for chemoreceptors
to try out the soil
prior to ovi-
position
the deed already done, she
is no longer as intensely
interested
in their scurrilous
song
or invigorating rhythms, per-
mutations of the D-S-C-H motif
reminiscent of
B
personal   A
signature   C
H
quoting bars from Galina's
Clarinet Trio in B-flat, mingling with
more agitation, more thrilling
counter-
point
One should hold off & gather
sense & sweetness
a whole life long, a long
life if possible, & then
right at the end
one could perhaps write
ten lines that are good

pressing for the tender
intimacy of humanist font
when everything is

        attacca

               after a pro-Palestinian rally
                       led to the
           vandalizing
                    & looting of Jewish
           businesses
                   & the burning

**At 9:10 a.m. an adult male was discovered
sitting on ground litter facing the sun in a
city lot**

       For the sake of a line of poetry one must see
       many cities, peoples, & things, one must know
       animals, must feel how the birds fly, & know
       the gestures with which small flowers open
       in the morning

            **At 9:13 a.m. the male began to stir
   & walked a short distance to a short
         grass,** *Buchloe*

               dactyloides

locals reported chants of "Gas
the Jews" & "Kill the Jews" as   *je*
rioters attacked businesses in   *suis*
the Sarcelles district known   *Shylock*
as "little Jerusalem"

        figures at the gathering exercise such politesse
        whirling, shaping cheeky sallies, exchanging
        obvious commentary like anywhere, really

but poetically, I have
just invented the

     flirt

        à

  deux

    **At 9:14 a.m. the male reached up with its mouthparts to the tip
    of a leaf & consumed the whole leaf to the base. He then attacked
    another leaf of the same plant, cutting it near the middle**

ghosts
    inhabit
        the clinically dispassionate Andantino, also without the
  sublime
     romance of the Second Quartet

including a kosher supermarket, a Jewish-owned
chemist & a funeral home. Rioters, who carried batons
& threw petrol
                    bombs
                              according to eyewitnesses, were
yards from the synagogue when they were
                    driven back by riot police who used
                                        tear
                              gas
through
        the open window & the spasmodic
        noises. But it is still not enough to
        have memories
                    Holding
on to the cut section with the front tarsi, he consumed all of it
from the cut end to the tip. He then cut another leaf of the same
plant near the base, held on to it with the front tarsi, & ate all of
it. A fourth
            & final leaf
                    was eaten from the tip to the
                                        base
returns to the charming élan
of the first movement, even
the social promiscuity
                    albeit oddly
        diminished
                    on the female's leathery tegmina
                    & drapes his abdomen over her
                                        right side
                    connecting in a J-shape
                    holding the edges of her saddle-like
                    pronotum with paired hooks on
                    prothoracic & mesothoracic
                                        legs
                    seizing ridges
                              then in the grip of passion, she
            walks
                    & jumps
                              for them both
not the memories themselves. Only when
they become blood in us, glance & gesture
nameless & no longer to be distinguished
from ourselves, only then can it happen

waking up one day as one of these intricate
insects & deeming it improvement, even a
red dragonfly eating dying leaves of may-
day
    tree

a most elegant refusal
closes over glacial pedal   hiding in
another thing written for the   Arcades
drawer, lest   Project!
    "musical circles
react to it negatively"

then in a very rare hour the first word of a line arises in their midst
& strides out of them
    Feeding ended at 9:24 a.m.

22

Flames
       I want to perpetuate each
               "ginch"
                     in wriggling box
                     next to droning
                     on of foaming
                     hive-
              mind
       on another Orwellian   "HATE"

but watch out what you share
Khrushchev still complains
about nausea & stomach
pain caused by that
          jazz
     concert
            scholars
            having traced
            referent to
            single purchase
            of
              "A" 22
                & 23
                  at ~~Upstart Crow~~
                    once above
                    decisive silver
                 undulations
                      of quay

poet living tomb of his
games — a quiet life for
an ocean: the *emphatical decussation*
quincunx **chiasma of 5-leafed, 5-**
blossomed, & of olive orchards
grenade bursts   tree
     murmuring with   >>> crickets <<<
         bees
where even as pen
spills, poems
        are falling
             into wide eyes
   (terrible
    poems!)
      & it is already too late
               for triage

that undulating
          accompaniment
                    like the chronicler
                              in *Boris Godunov*
                                        CONTEZ
               or relate what
                    splits heart to TELL
                                   casting out
                         the dark
                              circular
                                        D-
                                             S-
                                   C-
                                        H
                    without neuronal loophole
                    or break in hexagonal
                         cell
                              (or work station?)
sweeping aside motif (motive?)
               from Eighth String
          Quartet beloved
               in the West
                         (popular for general representation
                         of the futility of human endeavours)
in favour of poignant viola
                    solo
that homophonic
               texture
                                             so clear
               light incarnadine
                              quivers
                                        mid-
                                             air
               (dragon-
               fly or band-
               wing having   order
               eaten leaf   Odonata
               in the shape   *august*
               of a heart)   *tooth*
     while poems
               by drones
     are still falling
leaving little
          but flarf
               **YOU DON'T CARE
               ABOUT POETRY**

in the shape
of a tear-
gas cloud

Did I love a

dream?

public

installations

have nothing

on this crazed

polka

this time *inflections*

evoking propaganda
cartoons of Israelis
dancing around

missiles

bombs, etcetera

no worse than right-
wing media, right

I mean left, step to the
left &
flush left
then fall back into
line
understandably the long ostinato
broken by familiar fanfare
right out of *Guillaume*

Tell

You are hereby sentenced
to Al Purdy's house for
the time it takes to read
about Bruegel's babes
that became loaves
of bread (according to
ONE new Liverpudlian
at the BBC)

that sense of galloping away (No, Urban
with a bemused   Dictionary
Tonto   that's not
in tow   it at all!)

perpetuate these stereotypes
proud staples of our gross
domestic product
but

History's best emptied of names'
impertinence met on the ways

This visible
breath, ersatz
& serene

inspiration

evaporates

back to views

obscene

(from the rough

                Greek for be-
                        hind the scenes)
obscured, singing rivalry
songs in thick cattails, scraping   165 million
hard plectrum of one fore   years ago   (at the time
                        wing   nocturnal   of writing)
            against row   A.
                    of circular teeth   *musicus*
                            (file)   used a low-
on the underside of the   pitched
                    other   song
                wing

                                    inTerRuPteD
                                            by violent
                                    pizzicati
            but what if neuronal
            disorder won't pour
            so readily into
                            erasure
                        poetic
                                being a
            continually multiplying
                metaglut of information
                with the day manager
                                    gone
                                        fugal
            Inert   D-
                    every   S-
        thing burns   C-
                in this rusty   H
            hour
another
melancholy
recitative   this pattern
            another muffled   produced by a net-
                    concern   work of neurons in the
                        concern   central
                        nervous
                            system
                situated in the meta-
                thoracic
                        & anterior
                        abdominal
            portions
            of the ventral

nerve
cord
                                    seeking A-
        note
                        then will I wake to
            primitive
                        fever
        once again
                            erect
                    & alone
under an ancient flood
        of light
                (NO, no more of the cave-
                man stuff, honest injun!)
        but when this
        command
        neuron
                is active
        (based on sensory
                & hormonal
                    stimulation)
                        SAVAGE
                        VIOLIN
                                in the depths
                                of residential school
                            that first spark
                                of *Hammerklavier*
                            in his comely
                                        bones
        with apropos coda
        of classicist struggle
        by Silverman, our
        snazzy pianist:
                        Just try throwing a
                                rock
                    at a cop in this
                            country
        but when we have washed
        out our blood
            in cinemanic
        cliché
            we lie back
                on our stately laurels
                        [as in Ensoresque
                        illustration of the   Dumont

                              looting of Batoche   looking askance
                              lounging under sun   at Riel, some-
                              umbrella, lounging   where, too in-
                              through many a   decisive, too
                                        battle]   voice-riddled
              you just got to get when war makes sense   for
A   *attacca*

        sonorous

                vapid   when the going
                        monotonous line   was getting good

                        the country being full of 'em
                        so good for you
                        by good well-
                        meaning
                                        types
                        you have to perpetuate
                        these stereotypes

                                                    propaganda
                                                    cartoons falling
                buzzing like   out of German
                Virgil's eclogue   "echoes of Two-   bombers
                about appropriated   Gun   about Sam
                bee farm before he   Cohen"   Levy the arms-
                became a mouth-   dealing Jew
                piece for the   seducing
                        state   *THE GIRL*

                    YOU LEFT BEHIND
a   for a few bob
company   in league
            man   with the Yanks
                moving closer via
                phonotaxis, her ears
                in her front gams
                                respond most reliably
                                    to artificial stimuli
                matching her own
                    species' song
                                in sound
but when the Levy   frequency
brothers smuggled arms   & temporal
into Israel   pattern
                for a few bob   flying in
they were not exactly   formation for UK airshow, the pilot
treated like allies   behind

in American   killed them both
   POW   instantly
     camp
       (they would rather not have been
       flying Allied planes at all, would
       rather have been making
            & selling
      their dress
        designs)

           meanwhile, a knock-
           out in a new Anne
           Klein number
           sashays across &
           stomps
            all over
           Amazon
           book
            page

     but the main thing is to know
     what's right

I MEAN
LEFT

     to get back in your two cars
     comfortably above it all
     & horsepower
        away
         then maybe safely during a
        STOP
         light reach into snug shirt
        (made by
           someone else's brood)
 O *certain*   & post
 punishment ...   your vital sensitivity
         with a pretty
          device
        (made by
         someone else's
       brood)
because the main thing is everything
needs to be pretty
    hence these mowers
  grinding up
    styro-
   foam

but in this

exhilarating wind-

down

there can be

no more *morendo*

only the figure

of a

falling   one day we will ALL

semi-   stand in a circle

tone   jerk

linking all the movements   & have a

together   meme

No, the soul   made

emptied of   *this heavy*

words like leaky bin   *body must succumb*

over land-   *must remember to carry on*

fill   *through life in syrupy slumber*

23

Flame
directly after care in
neurological
unit
terra mutata
non mutat
mores
a train crosses the curvature of the earth in retinal attentiveness / levels prairie
a harbour of one's inner development
if you can believe such a glacial pace
stretches from
urban
wherever
a sense of alienation
at the edges
only the barest needs of communication will be allowed
me in society, I must live like an exile, if I come near people a hot
terror seizes me, a fear that my condition may be
noticed
antecedent melt-
down
to Eleventh String Quartet
in the key of
F minor (used by baroque
composers to indicate
death, heavy sorrow)
my former home
wealthy in
gelid
water
wobbly eclogue
returns in reams
of gov't bumf
not in the eye
of robin (nor aerial
shots
but closer to
ground   of cities we   droning
LEVEL   only fly over)   on
Forced already in early years to become a
philosopher, O, it is not easy, & harder
for an artist than another
how
relate disparate

                    histories
                        without getting
                                personal
        latrante uno
                latrat statim
                        et alter canis
                                yappy little lapdogs
                                along Victorian
                                notions of lawns
Eupolis
        devout in the school
                    of oppositional
                                poetics
        tossed into the sea
                    by Alcibiades
not quite able to
                pass
                    along his
                            disturbance
                                    of duty

a   During student elections in 1931, some 44.4 percent voted
wet   for the National Socialist German Students' League. In April
Vote   1933, the German Student Association conceived a campaign
or   called the "Action against the Un-German Spirit," & on April
Die!   12, it published its "12 Theses," which argued: "A Jew can only
T-shirt   think Jewish. If he writes in German, he is lying." This lie, the
gone wild   students continued, was to be "eradicated."

                                My father's farm
                                is still seized
                    How
                        about you help us
                        & we will help you
            Perhaps you could
                        enhance
                those pastorals
                        in the best
            interest of Rome
                        & we could
                                find you
                    a generous
                            patron
replies Gaius Asinius Pollio, allegedly

**where this final work of Mallarmé
testifies to his lifelong antipathy**

toward the current use of words
& the habitual
typography
of modern books
removed from the "scene"
more than I already was
amidst very well-deserved fierce criticism of the
Israeli government of which I am in full agreement with, it does feel very
alienating to see your "Friends" with gusto Liking comments that only
consist of
"Fucking Nazi Jews." Where do you go from there? Where can
you go? It's a vicious circle of rhetoric and violence
This is from academia
artists
poets & the like
Agnes Martin regards the material environment as transient and
exhaustible. Fueled by ego & pride & imprisoned in a never-
ending cycle of conquest & defeat, it is an illusory world of
shadows
& dreams
this bitter
& dissonant
flavour
fragments
into unsettling
"suites"
unless you're
a settler
suffers from
harmonic
dySfuNctIon
or blocked
fugues
bangs out the "wrong"
notes at chi-chi
receptions
It was no coincidence that she viewed music as the highest form
of art; with only eight notes & a completely abstract vocabulary,
musicians had expressed everything that had ever been
presumes *cri de coeur*
of failed capitalist
of failed "Indian"
or impoverished
mystic
even lacking *zutique*
backdoor in

                    this quadrant

                                        That chick in Swift
                                        Current will rob you!

if words were worth their weight
in derivative bushels
                    I would propose that

                                        Homer
                                                himself
                                        left no
                                                wealth
                                        after
                                                death

At an estimated cost of $12 billion, the project
would have created the largest linear particle
accelerator in the world & would likely have
provided years of employment for large numb-
ers of physicists in the United States. But after
the cancellation, the job market for academic
physicists collapsed and many moved into
finance
                    & quantitative

                                analysis
        Flashes of awareness are para-
verbal; they occur in the emotional or intuitional sphere
which Martin calls the inner mind

                                with the first violin-driving scherzo
                                with repetitive
                                                Fs

until it runs out of steam
                        utterly
                                spent
                                        on this interminable plain

        we give a whirl on white-
        board as tranquil
                        inner
                                landscape

                                        when you're toes-up
                                        it's what the market
                                                will bear

                but one aspect
                        of his so-called
                hermeticism
                        is in the meticulous
                                        care
                he always brought to the

                                        physical
                    appearance of his
                                poems
    to the silences

    of the margins

                    & the blank
                            pages
                                limbs
                                    loose
                            with slumber
                    where false dreams
                                linger
                    countless as
                                ears
                    of harvest
                                corn
                                illimitable
                                            as grains
                                of sand
        since the train
        of thought
        is chocka-
        block with
        uranium
                    et ibant obscuri sola

                            sub nocte per umbram
                                            GO RIDERS GO

            The universe
                        of traded products grew dramatically
        with only a few
    setbacks: for example, the Orange
     County debacle in 1994
                            & the Russian debt crisis
                & collapse
                        of Long-Term
    Capital
            Management
                    in 1998
    where such a harsh
    recitative is relieved
                    by that tiny
                            tornado
                                of an étude   where

"blanks"

indeed take on IMPORTANCE
where versification
necessitates
        a   surrounding

a fragment, lyrical   silence

or of a few beats

          occupies

               Martin's parents homesteaded a farm in Maklin, northern Saskatchewan, where they grew wheat, the dominant crop of Canada's agricultural heartland. It was here that Martin developed an appreciation for the continuum & rhythms of nature & for unencumbered, boundless spaces demarcated by the man-made geometries of roads   & rows of   wheat

but we regret to inform
you funding has been
        DENIED
   for a
      humoresque

            Lucky old man
        so your land
    will remain
          & large enough for you
    though wholly dressed
         with naked stone
    though filthy marsh
         suffuses your pasture with reeds
  Still, nothing strange
       & dangerous
         will attack
   your breeding food
       nor will cattle
     of rich
       neighbours
         corrupt them

in 1943 she escaped while in transport
to a Dutch "transit camp" for Auschwitz-
Birkenau to
     drown herself
          in that way   she didn't give
them the satisfaction. My maternal ancestors too
escaped pogroms in Eastern Europe
before settling
     Most "converted" before
          WW2
& thought they were safe
     but they were
          not
Once, when one of her paintings received a major
          scrape,   she
resisted restoring it, declaring that accidents were part of nature
& thus intrinsic to the work. Nor did she feel that she could take
credit for her art. She was an intermediary, the locus for the work's
occurrence; she was no more responsible for it than a potato farmer
was for his crop
     Lucky old man
          here by mapped rivers
     & sacred springs
          you will long
     for cool shade
From now on
     & forever
          beside every fence
willow blossoms
     swarmed
          by Hybla's
     bees
     will often
urge you on
     with murmurs
          to drowsing
here
     beneath fortifications
          where the pruner will sing
          into the wind
& hoarse pigeons
     will not perish
(your worry)
     & mourning
     dove
     will not stop
     lamenting from

                              nearby
                                 elm
      For poetry will always remain an out-
      sider, & its trembling flights to places other than the page
      are no more than parodied by the span of the hasty or vast page
      of the newspaper
                              ~~we hold in our hands~~

speaking of Li Po
                        or Cavalcanti (no lunar
                                    embrace
                                    or golden
                                    shower
                                             for them

            more quick-
            sand
                      quag-
            mire
                        alluding to state propaganda
                              or anti-heretical
                                    dictates
~~our reason alone should warn us that harm done our fellows can~~
~~never bring happiness to us; & our heart, that contributing to~~
~~their felicity is the greatest joy Nature has accorded us on earth;~~
~~the entirety of human morals is contained in this one phrase:~~
~~*Render others as happy as one desires oneself to be, & never*~~
~~*inflict more pain upon them than one would like to receive at*~~
~~their hands. There you are, my friend, those are the only~~
~~principles we should observe, & you need neither god nor~~
~~religion to appreciate and subscribe to them, you need only~~
~~have~~
            a good heart
                        or the irregular rhythms
                                          of Mahler's
                                                    in his Ninth

Symphony
            & here
                        is the emotional
            heart
                        of the quartet
                              concern regarding what I perceived to be an influx
                              of anti-Semitic tendencies online & elsewhere
                              then he accused me of
                                          "being tribal"

            then let our "safe-
word" in continual times   I
of trouble   don't

be   Like
    "Passamaquoddy"   this
            sinking
                into slough
where the history
        of a thought
            is like the history
                    of a speculation
    imperilled at every
                moment
                    & at every
                        place
forget your gods
            ~~& your religions too: they are none of them~~
    ~~good for anything but to set man at odds with man, & the mere~~
    ~~name of these horrors has caused greater loss of life on earth~~
    ~~than all other wars and all other plagues combined. Renounce~~
    ~~the idea of another world; there is none, but do not renounce~~
    ~~the pleasure of being happy & of making for happiness in this~~
Nature offers you
            no other
                way
    I would stay in bed until the late afternoon sometimes
    waiting for inspiration so I could get up & paint. Then I would
            start painting & be interrupted by a
                            phone call or visitor. When I
            went back to the painting I would not have an idea of
what my inspiration
                was
                    souls
                astir
        in begging
            bowl
                the breath
                        of such flatness
                            is cold & cruel
                                    here at the edge
                            of metropolis
are you ragged
        wayward in walking
                    friend of old
        remember
                Henan
                where you read
                        my poems
        beware of

brilliant

      moons

           dancing in

                  rivers

            of cloud

autumnal   THE HUBRIS OF

     mud   SASKATCHEWAN

        biting   FOOT

          your boots

                not blood

                     be not

                       blood

but before Prokofiev's Sarcasms
perhaps we meet at some 1920s
speakeasy
        & stumble on a little
  Franck
      say, a sonata
            passionately dissected
                  by Proust
     as symptomatic
          of strained love
   in a beastly
        world
        I feel cornered in a position, with calls for
        "Jews of conscience" to speak out. Proof
        that you are a good Jew! It's more like an
        ongoing snuff film festival now, with dead
        bodies posted constantly
still locked into a vocabulary that describes the insular drops of rain
rather than their interstices

                  & yes, like Swann
                  feeling poorly
                  in later volumes
                  we could sharpen
                  our views
                        on the
                      Dreyfus
                        Affair

roughly 40,000 people were
standing in the pouring rain
at Opernplatz square in Berlin
to see how this could be done.
They included Erich Kästner,
who would later call Goebbels
a "little limping devil" & a

"failed human being." Kästner
had come to watch his own
                         books being burned, especially "Fabian,"
            which the Nazi Party newspaper *Völkischer Beobachter* called
            a "dirty tale," filled with "descriptions of sub-
                                                    human orgies."
            friend of old
                        sent
                                    downriver
                                                with the prince
smiling
            ironically
                        at town folk
                                    until
                                    Yangzhou
the divide
            of death
                        encourages
                                    angst
            I suppose you could say I wasn't up to the demands &
            everything, the life I had to live there. But there was
            something else; that I came to a place of recognition
            of confusion that had to be solved. I had to have time
            & nobody's going to give you time
                                                where I was
                        So I had to leave
            Jiangnan
                        O plagued country
where
            an outcast
                        is hardly fresh
                                    news
as the leaves of autumn fall
                                    & are withered
                        so hope
                                    has been blighted, almost as I arrive
I go away
                        guessing why
                        Klimt made
                        Mahler the hero of his
                        Beethoven Frieze
                                    once again presenting to academic
                        panel
                                    "unclear ideas through
                                                unclear forms"
                                                            old friend

                                        deep
                                    in dream
                                                you
                                        are clear
                                remember me
                are your feathered
                                    plumes
                pinioned
                            by thick nets
                                        such
                                        dread
        the road far
                            completely unknown
                soul
                    leaving green
                                maples
                        returning
                            to dark
                                    wood
        drowned
                    within flood
                                of moonlight
        within beams
                    of roof
                        light of
                                doubt
                                    shed upon
                                            your face
                where the drink
                                is deep
                awash
                        with thirsty
                                    waves
                                beware death
                                    by water beast
exactly what a modern person demands:
            a reflection, of whatever sort – served by that obsequious
        phantom woven of the
                                word that is ready for every occasion
            but hoarse raven
                        lean coyotes
            what has come
                    over you
        dream
            . *are you near*
                        or is your

soul
      a peacock fan
           of plumes
              a roar
                 of familiar
            fumes
     Kästner, who is now chiefly known as a writer
           of children's books, did indeed describe
        quick
    sex, casual sex & lesbian sex, in addition to love bought
& sold, desire & suicide, unfaithful spouses, the tender
                juggernaut
of modernity, newspaper editorial offices full of opportunists, dance
halls full of lunatics, &
       a city filled with
          beggars, brothels
             & chaos
     with sinking
        mind
         held down
           by sleep
where hungry
    ghosts
      whistle through
         divided
          valleys
  of falling
    light
      orange
        sighs
         friend of old

Rectangular
in format, these
grids established
"a sort of contra-
diction, a dis-
sonance" in r-
elation to the
square format
of the paintings
that "lightens
the weight of
the square &
destroys
its power"

then by the Ides

of March
                    the prince put
                                to death
& you
        friend of old
                    bound
                        & banished
                                    to malarial
                                            Guizhou
        have you
            fled
                    those contaminated
                                waters
                                        of Yelang
                                                yet
"surely the people is grass,"
says a coal scorching lips in a
        charming image in a
            forgotten book
                            while outside Walmart, a mother
                                unwraps endless packaging &
                                    slaps it upon overflowing bin
                            more fodder for the mowers
                            of gov't summer workers (?)
                            more entanglements for wilds
                            on environmental reserve
                            the thing itself a dreamy truck
                            handed directly to her kid
                            presumably tricked out in
                            lead paint
                                        but most certainly
                        made in ~~China~~
                        Taiwan
                                (by another tyke?)
            VITA
                    SINE
        LIBRIS
                    MORS
                        EST
day-long
        clouds
                are adrift
                                    the drifter
                        long since
                                late
    three nights

                    dreaming afresh
                              of your kindly
        mind
              heavy with
                        friends
                              & farewells
              tangled
                    rushes
        a bitter trip
                    water whipped
                              by wind whorl
        the oars
              wary of ship-
                        wreck
                    Their meeting takes place
                         an influence
                    under   **alien I know**
                    that of Music
                              heard in concert
              one finds there
              several techniques
                    that belong
                         to Literature
                              I reclaim
                                   them

        a subtle
              unevenness — a
                    "visual tremolo"
        but you left
              scratching
                    furrowed
                         head
        shaken
              by fate

                    while solar roofs
                         shadow city hall
              contemporaries, like stubborn mules, are running
        backwards toward a yawning abyss in which there is enough room
        for all the nations
        of Europe   like a number of others before and alongside him, he
        cries out:
                              Watch out! Grip the handrail on your
        left with your
        left hand!
                    these men alone

are wretched

but is the mesh

of heaven

broad

enough

when the names

of autumnal

armies

are sung alone

when life is done

frigid

wind

scaling the end

of the world

ideas

no things   *in*

but in   *things*

Ikea   *their*

own

elite

With the depiction of unattached emotions came
the feeling that she was no longer

subliminally veiling

personal feelings or holding

the chaos of the world

at bay

waiting for

crooked-necked

geese

yet how

autumn

floods the waters

yet how

literature

hates those

favoured

by fate

mountain

devils

wait for

faults

**The discredit in which the book trade has
placed itself is associated less with a cessation
of its operations, of which I find no sign, than
with its notorious impotence when faced with
works of exceptional**

worth

you must speak
          with the wronged
soul
    leaving poems
              in the
                    Miluo
                                        remember
                              Chu Yuan
                                    was exiled
                              by the king
                                        of Chu
          his rivals
                    strived
                        & spat lies
                                    driving him
          to drowning
                    in the
                              Miluo

Martin readily acknowledged
that the condition of interior
solitude which her paintings
required might prevent some
viewers from appreciating
                    them

a century hence
              it was Han poet
                    Jia Yi
                        who let loose
                                    a bundle
                              of verse
                                        like leaves
                              or falling
                                    light
                    into the
                              Miluo
    upon the
              uneven
                    altar
                        of Chu Yuan
                              on his way
                        to banishment
                              in Changsha
hunt

      & peck frantically
                        for acceptable
poetic
              representation of
              reclaimed
                      leopard
           frog
with the
         brekekekex ko-ax ko-ax
                     brekekekex ko-ax ko-ax
already
        old hat
           & unsustained
                  rather like Beckett's
          Watt having break-
    down
           over frog chorus

Krak!   ____   ____   ____   ____   ____   ____   ____
Krek!   ____   ____   ____   ____ Krek!   ____   ____
____ Krik!   ____   ____ Krik!   ____   ____ Krik!

but by the last
           movement
                  everything is
                        organic
      save that the first
              violin
            holds a high C
                    for nearly
                          thirty seconds

a-
  kin to Eugen Gomringer's

Beau Dick,   burning
his own Kwakwaka'wakw
masks outside hip
hop exhibit

significance

to each

their own

Rothko's
Chapel

before
a   soft   sustained   scream   of   anguish   dissolves   into

pitiless

space

24

NEVER

A clear night   if the mind were clear

mostly composition
composition that's the whole thing

DEPTHS OF
SHIPWRECK

You will not think

form,   space,   line,   contour

Abyss
bleached

desperately
a wing
of its
own

Beauty is
pervasive

resumes in interior
shadow engulfed by depth
by that alternative
sail

If the mind were clear
you could take this mind

this particular
                    state

        cannot   be another

                                                        relinquish

cleaving

in the name of the waves

                This painting I like because you can get in there
                                                    & rest

        this is what is possible

                        ancestrally never to open
                                        fist
                                        tightened
                                        over use-
                                        less head

                    what comes to you free is enlightening

                            MISSING
                claim ~~disappearance~~
                                    to some-
                                        body

                                            ambiguous

for which the mind is famous

                hard   bone   lost   between   the   planks

I believe in the recurrence

Engagements

Before paper

    it exists in the mind

    phantom
        of a
           gesture

                        NEVER TO

ABOLISH

    The untroubled mind

        to which complication of the involved life
        is like chaos

AS IF

    An insinuation
    in silence

        look in my mind for the unwritten page

  A clear
    night
     in which two planets
seem to clasp

tornado
whirlwind of hilarity
& horror
churns   around the gulf

our responses are s(t)imulated

AS IF

you're just like me

a lone
plume
overwhelmed

It's consolation

that rigid non-colour

derisory
called this rock up out of the mud
turned into a rock
summoned a vision of

quiet

in bolt out of blue

grass
thought the wind
great comfort

mute   laughter

over

IF

      lamp   ink   window

                When
                We should tell the wind our gratitude

impatient ultimate scales   bifurcate

                We are ineffectual

                    imposed
                        capped the infinite

bringing thoughts to the surface
                of my mind
                    I can watch
      them
          dissolve

                        FATIDIC

a sustained note
        from each *Orchelimum gladiator*
                fills ear
                  pours
            into pre-
        occupations

      stellar
      issue   up again

makes itself up, rushes forth getting
          up again   nowhere really
crashes, withdraws, makes itself

                  in the original froth

before   we
were   separate
so   insular

NOTHING
    of the memorable crisis
        where the event   up
           swelled

                  I do not exist
no thinking of others even when they are there, no interruption

    amid these vague
        waves
           in which all reality

                  di sol es
                   s   v

    giving up everything

      in accord with such obliquity via such declivity

             of fire

As long as I look in my mind
      & see nothing at all

            A CONSTELLATION
        cold from neglect & desuetude

It is very pleasant

    The all of all,   reality,   mind   sidereally

All thought emits

O
    to reach you at last,   what a strange path
                                    I had to take

Acknowledgements

A moment of silence for Ralph Maud (1928–2014), whose scholarship on Charles Olson and West Coast First Nations ethnography, along with his pivotal gift of a pamphlet entitled *The Horn of Ulf*, have gone a long way towards laying the groundwork for books like and including this one.

Thank you to everyone at Talonbooks, especially Gregory Gibson for taking time from his new career to expertly oversee the seventh title we have done together. Warm thanks also to Michael Barnholden, whose editorial suggestions and key Saskatchewanianisms greatly improved this book. Special thanks also to Leslie Thomas Smith for his careful recreation of the original text.

Thank you to Smaro Kamboureli, whose generous supply of critical writings and materials on the contemporary long poem has certainly helped me to cultivate an imaginary allotment, so to speak.

Thank you to Dan L. Johnson, professor of environmental science at the University of Lethbridge, who is always on call to help with identifications of anything orthopteran, and who definitely helped me to become a grasshopper buff.

Thank you to *BathHouse Journal*, *The Capilano Review*, *The Puritan*, and Penguin Random House Canada, for publishing poems from this book.

Thank you, friends, for howling over the lonesome gusts of my continual prairie quest.

Garry Thomas Morse's nine book titles include a poetic explo-
ration of his mother's Kwakwaka'wakw First Nations ancestry
in *Discovery Passages*, finalist for the Governor General's Award
for Poetry and the Dorothy Livesay Poetry Prize. *Discovery Pas-
sages* was also voted One of the Top Ten Poetry Collections of 2011
by the *Globe and Mail*, One of the Best Ten Aboriginal Books from
the past decade by CBC's *8th Fire*, and was recommended by the
2014 First Nations Communities Read program for public libraries
across the nation.

Morse's books of fiction include his story collection *Death in
Vancouver*, and the three books in his outlandish genre-warping
Chaos! Quincunx series, including 2013 ReLit Award final-
ist *Minor Episodes / Major Ruckus*, 2014 ReLit Award finalist
Rogue Cells / Carbon Harbour, and a time travel romp called *Minor
Expectations*, all published by Talonbooks.

After a year and a half of deep contemplation in the company of
remarkable jackrabbits and grasshoppers in Regina, Saskatchewan,
Morse has recently claimed new territory in Winnipeg, Manitoba.
The result is the book you are holding.